‖‖‖ ‖‖‖‖‖‖ ‖ ‖‖ ‖‖‖‖‖‖‖ ‖‖ ‖‖

W9-DBI-696

SECURITIES MARKETS AND SYSTEMIC RISKS IN DYNAMIC ASIAN ECONOMIES

Dr S. Ghon Rhee
Director
Pacific-Basin Capital Markets Research Center
University of Rhode Island

NO LONGER THE PROPERTY
OF THE
UNIVERSITY OF R. I. LIBRARY

ORGANISATION FOR ECONOMIC CO-OPERATION AND DEVELOPMENT

ORGANISATION FOR ECONOMIC CO-OPERATION AND DEVELOPMENT

Pursuant to Article 1 of the Convention signed in Paris on 14th December 1960, and which came into force on 30th September 1961, the Organisation for Economic Co-operation and Development (OECD) shall promote policies designed:

— to achieve the highest sustainable economic growth and employment and a rising standard of living in Member countries, while maintaining financial stability, and thus to contribute to the development of the world economy;
— to contribute to sound economic expansion in Member as well as non-member countries in the process of economic development; and
— to contribute to the expansion of world trade on a multilateral, non-discriminatory basis in accordance with international obligations.

The original Member countries of the OECD are Austria, Belgium, Canada, Denmark, France, Germany, Greece, Iceland, Ireland, Italy, Luxembourg, the Netherlands, Norway, Portugal, Spain, Sweden, Switzerland, Turkey, the United Kingdom and the United States. The following countries became Members subsequently through accession at the dates indicated hereafter: Japan (28th April 1964), Finland (28th January 1969), Australia (7th June 1971) and New Zealand (29th May 1973). The Commission of the European Communities takes part in the work of the OECD (Article 13 of the OECD Convention). Yugoslavia has a special status at OECD (agreement of 28th October 1961).

Publié en français sous le titre :

MARCHÉS BOURSIERS ET RISQUES SYSTÉMIQUES
DANS LES ÉCONOMIES DYNAMIQUES D'ASIE

THE OPINIONS EXPRESSED AND ARGUMENTS EMPLOYED IN THIS PUBLICATION ARE THE SOLE RESPONSIBILITY OF THE AUTHOR AND DO NOT NECESSARILY REFLECT THOSE OF THE OECD OR OF THE GOVERNMENTS OF ITS MEMBER COUNTRIES

© OECD 1992
Applications for permission to reproduce or translate all or part of this publication should be made to:
Head of Publications Service, OECD
2, rue André-Pascal, 75775 PARIS CEDEX 16, France

Foreword

As part of the ongoing informal dialogue between the Organisation for Economic Co-Operation and Development (OECD) countries and six Dynamic Asian Economies (DAEs), including Hong Kong, Korea, Malaysia, Singapore, Taiwan and Thailand, the OECD organised a workshop on 6th-7th May 1991, in Singapore. The main theme of this workshop was: "Organisation and Regulation of Securities Markets in Six DAEs." The OECD requested the author to prepare a report entitled "Systemic Risks in Securities Markets of Six Dynamic Asian Economies," which was to be used as a discussion document at the OECD/DAE Workshop. According to an OECD mandate, this report has been designed to: (a) analyse structures and mechanisms of securities markets in the six DAEs; (b) identify main issues and problems related to the systemic risks in these markets; and (c) analyse the arrangements for supervision. This report has also been guided by an OECD report entitled *Systemic Risks in Securities Markets*, which was completed by the OECD ad hoc Group of Experts on Securities Markets and published by OECD in February 1991.

The author visited the OECD in Paris on 14th and 15th January 1991 to define the scope of the proposed report with members of the OECD staff. In preparation for this report, the author also visited five DAEs (Hong Kong, Korea, Malaysia, Singapore, and Thailand) from 16th February to 6th March 1991. During his visits, the author met representatives of organisations of the five DAEs, which have been listed in Annex 1.

On 21st June 1991, this report was presented to the Committee on Financial Markets, which recommended its publication on the responsibility of the Secretary-General of the OECD.

The views expressed in this report are those of the author and do not necessarily reflect those of the OECD, nor of its Member Governments.

ALSO AVAILABLE

Bank Profitability . Statistical Supplement – Financial Statements of Banks 1981-1989 (1991)
(21 91 03 3) ISBN 92-64-03518-4   FF150   £21.00   US$38.00   DM62

Financial Market Trends

No. 47. Special Feature: Financial Systems and Financial Regulations in Dynamic Asian Economies. (1990)
(27 90 03 1)
Per issue   FF80   £10.00   US$17.00   DM33

Systemic Risks in Securities Markets (1991)
(21 91 01 1) ISBN 92-64-13454-9   FF100   £12.00   US$21.00   DM39

Trends in Banking Structure and Regulation in OECD Countries

Competition in Banking *by G. Bröker* (1989)
(21 89 01 1) ISBN 92-64-13197-3   FF195   £23.50   US$41.00   DM80

Prices charged at the OECD Bookshop.
THE OECD CATALOGUE OF PUBLICATIONS and supplements will be sent free of charge
on request addressed either to OECD Publications Service,
or to the OECD Distributor in your country.

Contents

Explanatory notes

1. Currency equivalents: US$1.00
   (As of December 1989)

Hong Kong	HK$7.80
Korea	W 675.02
Malaysia	M$2.70
Singapore	S$1.90
Taiwan	NT$26.17
Thailand	B 25.18

2. The term "billion" signifies a thousand million.

3. The following abbreviations and acronyms appear in this report:

ADR	American Depositary Receipt
ANC	Adjusted Net Capital
ASSET	Automated System Stock Exchange of Thailand
BOT	Bank of Thailand
BSE	Bumiputera Stock Exchange or Pasaran Saham Bumiputera
CATS	Computer-Assisted Trading System
CBOT	Chicago Board of Trade
CDP	Central Depository Pte Ltd.
CFTC	Commodity Futures Trading Commission
CLOB	Central Limit Order Book
CIC	Capital Issues Committee
CME	Chicago Mercantile Exchange
DAE	Dynamic Asian Economy
DJIA	Dow-Jones Industrial Average
DOT	Designated Order Turnaround System
DTC	Depository Trust Company
DVP	Delivery versus Payment

EEC	European Economic Community
FRBNY	Federal Reserve Bank of New York
G-30	Group of Thirty
FDSS	Fixed Delivery and Settlement System
FGC	Hong Kong Futures Guarantee Corporation
FHSFC	Fuh-Hwa Securities Finance Company
FIBV	Fédération Internationale des Bourses de Valeurs
FIC	Foreign Investment Committee
HKCC	HKFE Clearing Corporation Ltd.
HKFE	Hong Kong Futures Exchange Ltd.
HKSCC	Hong Kong Securities Clearing Co., Ltd.
ICCH	International Commodities Clearing House
IDAS	Institutional Delivery and Affirmation System
IDR	International Depositary Receipt
IOSCO	International Organisation of Securities Commissions
ISE	International Stock Exchange
ISIN	International Securities Identification Number
ISO	International Organisation for Standardisation
ISSA	International Society of Securities Administrators
JCF	Joint Compensation Fund
JSCC	Japan Securities Clearing Corporation
KLSE	Kuala Lumpur Stock Exchange
KSDA	Korean Securities Dealers Association
KSE	Korea Stock Exchange
KSFC	Korea Securities Finance Corporation
KSSC	Korea Securities Settlement Corporation
MAS	Monetary Authority of Singapore
MCD	Malaysian Central Depository Sdn. Bhd.
MOF	Ministry of Finance
MOS	Mutual Offset System
NASD	National Association of Securities Dealers
NASDAQ	NASD Automated Quotation system
NBER	National Bureau of Economic Research
NSCC	National Securities Clearing Corporation
NYSE	New York Stock Exchange

OECD	Organisation for Economic Co-Operation and Development
OTC	Over-the-counter
RAES	Retail Automated Exchange System
ROC	Registrar of Companies
S&P	Standard and Poor's
SCANS	Securities Clearing Automated Network Services Sdn. Bhd.
SCCS	Securities Clearing and Computer Services (Pte) Ltd.
SCORE	System On Computerised Order Routing and Execution
SDC	Share Depository Center
SEC	Securities & Exchange Commission or Securities Exchange Commission
SEHK	Stock Exchange of Hong Kong Ltd.
SES	Stock Exchange of Singapore
SESDAQ	Stock Exchange of Singapore Dealing and Automated Quotation
SET	Stock Exchange of Thailand
SIMEX	Singapore International Monetary Exchange
SFC	Securities & Futures Commission
SMATS	Stock Market Automated Trading System
SOES	Small Order Execution System
SRC	Securities Review Commission
TOP	Panel on Take-overs and Mergers
TSCD	Taiwan Securities Central Depository Co., Ltd.
TSE	Tokyo Stock Exchange
TSEC	Taiwan Stock Exchange Corporation

Chapter I

Scope of the Project and Terms of Reference

The main objective of this report is to examine the organisation and regulation of securities markets in the six DAEs. The report focuses on the main issues contained in the OECD's report *Systemic Risks in Securities Markets* (referred to as "Systemic Risks Report", 1991). Specifically, the following issues should be addressed in three major areas relevant to the securities markets in the six DAEs.

Market mechanisms

a) market mechanisms employed by the DAEs to contain systemic risks and to prevent the spreading of such risks to other markets;

b) numerous measures adopted by DAEs for increase in trading capacity, regulation of programme trading, circuit breakers, and improvement of clearing and settlement systems;

c) the impact of trading automation on systemic risks in DAEs and new challenges posed by this automation; and

d) serious deficiencies in the present market mechanisms of the DAEs.

Securities market regulation

a) main features of and gaps in the supervisory coverage of DAEs' securities firms;

b) the development of proper capital adequacy standards for securities firms;

c) new issues posed by the breakdown of barriers between financial market segments; and

d) co-operative arrangements between securities market regulators in the Asian region and beyond.

Integration of DAEs' securities markets in the global financial system

    a)   main consequences of integrating DAEs' securities markets in the global financial system through liberalisation and cross-border listing; and

    b)   implications for systemic risks.

This report has the following limitations in scope: first, short-term money markets and bond markets are not covered unless they pose issues relevant to the overall scope of the report as defined by detailed terms of reference; second, the coverage of this report is limited to equity markets and securities companies. As a result, detailed analyses of the economy of each of the six DAEs and non-securities market financial institutions such as commercial and development banks are not given; and third, the equity derivative markets of the six DAEs are discussed only when they are related to systemic risks in the equity markets of the six DAEs since the majority of the six DAEs do not have fully developed markets for equity derivative products. Hence, detailed regulatory arrangements and related discussions of the equity derivative markets are covered when relevant to the discussions of the equity markets.

Chapter II

Systemic risks

For the purpose of this report, it should be appropriate to introduce the concept of *systemic risks* as defined by the Systemic Risks Report (1991). The Systemic Risks Report defines *systemic crisis* as a disturbance impairing the working of the system which is composed of market participants, trading mechanisms, clearing and settlement arrangements, regulatory arrangements, etc. *Systemic risks* are those risks with the potential to cause such a crisis and, in extreme cases, a breakdown in the system. In the Systemic Risks Report, systemic risks in national securities markets are examined primarily as components of the international securities markets. An increasing body of literature on the stock market crash examined issues related to stock market volatility, the impact of trading equity derivative products on the cash market, market structures, clearing and settlement systems, and standardization of regulatory processes, without a general definition of systemic risks and without delineating directions for future research. The Systemic Risks Report provides securities industry practitioners and academicians with a much needed perspective which has been lacking in numerous recent studies.

O'Connor (1989) introduced two types of market efficiency: informational efficiency and operational efficiency. The former implies that securities prices fully reflect all available information relevant to determining their value, while the latter requires that intermediaries channel funds in an optimal manner. Taking operational efficiency as given, modern finance theory concentrated on the informational efficiency of securities markets. In retrospect, one obvious contribution made by the 1987 market break was that both practitioners and academicians realised that operational efficiency could not be taken for granted and further that the aggregate cost of failure in the operating system of securities markets might be as large as or even larger than the social costs associated with informationally inefficient markets.

Corrigan's (1989) speech delivered at the National Bureau of Economic Research (NBER) Conference on "Reducing the Risk of Economic Crisis" touched upon the question of systemic risks. He observed a greater number of financial disruptions with potential systemic implications over the past 15 years than over the entire postwar period prior to 1974. He cited three reasons for these disruptions: (a) macroeconomic policies and performance with particular reference to US budget deficits, public and private debt, and inflation; (b) financial innovation and technological advances in securities markets; and (c) heavy emphasis on short-term returns and rewards. In his diagnosis of recent financial disruptions, Corrigan identified the following common denominators. First, financial institutions concentrated their activities or exposures. Concentrations took many forms: exposures to a single borrower, exposures to a single industry, exposures to a single instrument, exposures to a single class of borrowers, or exposures to single commodity. Second, Corrigan observed the so-called "bandwagon" effect. Financial innovations that initially produce high rates of return for the innovator tend to be very short-lived in the financial sector because they are easy to duplicate. However, the "bandwagon" effect, reinforced by the illusions of permanent high rates of return and liquidity, tends to draw relatively unsophisticated players into such activities at just the wrong time. Third, there has been a threat of dislocation in payment, settlement, or clearing systems. Payment and settlement systems are of special importance because such systems can act as the vehicle through which a localised problem can be very quickly transmitted to other markets, thereby taking on systemic implications. Fourth, some segments of financial markets may be characterised by a condition of overcrowding such that spreads and returns do not fully compensate for risks. Corrigan cited the fifth denominator as supervisory gaps or breakdowns in the supervisory process.[1] Corrigan's common denominators represent potential weaknesses in the operating system of securities markets. One or multiple weaknesses may unexpectedly erupt in a small securities company in the form of payment default. This default may cause a contagious panic among securities firms or among markets.[2]

The policy issue is how to manage systemic risks under the existing arrangements and how to improve present operating systems in securities markets. This report will examine the current status of operating systems of securities markets in the six DAEs, focusing initially on the operating efficiency of the DAEs' securities markets against the backdrop of the 1987 market crash. The issues relevant to systemic risks span a wide range of topics, including market volatility, market mechanisms, clearing and settlement systems, margin regulations, regulation gaps, and capital adequacy of securities firms.

Chapter III

Market volatility

Stock market volatility has been one of the most researched topics since the market crash of 1987. The Market Volatility and Investor Confidence Panel created by the New York Stock Exchange (NYSE) (to be referred to as the Smith Panel) correctly pointed out that stock market volatility means different things to different people. Academicians use the statistical variability to define market volatility, while investors and regulators seem more worried about extreme intra-day price movements which may have very little to do with stock fundamentals. Schwert (1990) introduced two versions of volatility, depending upon the length of time over which the volatility is measured: (a) long-horizon volatility; and (b) short-horizon volatility, including intra-day volatility. According to Schwert, long-horizon volatility is determined by corporate financial and operating leverage, personal leverage, and business conditions. Unfortunately, the determinants of short-horizon volatility are unknown and controversial. Two major themes of investigation in a number of studies initiated by regulatory agencies in the United States, the United Kingdom, Hong Kong, and in numerous academic research papers include: (a) inter-market volatility transmission; and (b) the relationship between the equity derivative markets and the equity market.

A. Inter-market volatility transmission

Numerous academic papers examined the question of inter-market volatility transmission after the 1987 market crash. Kelleher (1988) reported that stock price movements in major markets in the world became increasingly similar in the 1980s, compared to the 1970s and before. This development appears consistent with the ongoing strengthening of cross-border trading, listing, and investment activities. Empirical results reported by King and Wadhwani (1990) perhaps provide the most convincing evidence in support of the interdependence of national securities markets. Their results indicate that the opening of the NYSE was associated with unusually high market volatility in London and, further, that market volatility in London was lower when the New York market was closed some Wednesdays in 1968 to clear the settlement backlog. They attributed these results to the informational role of prices and the extent to which investors as well as market makers in one country's stock market rationally infer information about the value of their equities observing the price of foreign stocks on foreign stock markets. Hamao, Masulis, and Ng (1990) also document important empirical evidence of a significant volatility spill-over effect from New York to Tokyo, London to Tokyo, and New York to London, which is consistent with the theory of inter-market volatility transmission.[3,4] Hamao, Masulis, and Ng (1991) analysed daily open-to-close returns from the three major stock exchanges over a five year period that includes the October 1987 market crash. They found some evidence that volatility spill-over effects emanating from Japan have been gathering strength over time, and this trend appear more pronounced following the 1987 market crash. From these results, it appears that a large price decline in one major market could trigger a serious disruption in another market and, eventually, in the global financial system through volatility transmission or the spill-over effect. This conclusion raises an interesting challenge for regulators of securities markets because the interdependence of national securities markets will place strains on global supervisory efforts. Internationally co-ordinated efforts will be more important than ever. The cross-border co-ordination of circuit breaker systems and margin regulations, if they turn out to be effective in controlling the excessive volatility, will be needed. The standardization of clearing and settlement systems, listing requirements, and disclosure requirements will also be useful to augment the effectiveness of the global financial system.

A recent study by Ng, Chang, and Chou (1990) reported that cross-border equity investment is an important factor in explaining the transmission of market volatility from one national market to another. They found no volatility spill-over from the US market to Korea and Taiwan, which are effectively closed to cross-border investment. No spill-over was found from the US market to Thailand prior to September 1987 when the SET opened an alien board to facilitate the trading of Thai securities by foreign investors. Additionally, volatility spill-over from the US market to Japan occurred mostly after US securities firms were allowed to become members of the Tokyo Stock Exchange (TSE) in February 1986. These results are supported by Park and Fatemi (1991) who examined the linkages between smaller Asian markets and larger developed markets in New York, London, and Tokyo. The Park and Fatemi findings suggest that the Australian market exhibits a relatively strong linkage to the developed markets; Hong Kong, New Zealand, and Singapore exhibit moderate linkages; and Korea, Taiwan, and Thailand exhibit little linkage to these markets. This result is somewhat surprising considering their strong economic ties with major developed countries, but it may be explained, in part, by the extent of market liberalisation, the degree of foreign exchange control, and the stages of market development.

Of the six DAEs, securities markets in Korea, Taiwan, and Thailand have yet to be opened. In fact, all three countries are in the process of liberalising and/or internationalising their securities markets. Recently, Taiwan's government permitted foreign institutional investors, including banks, insurance companies, and fund management firms, to invest directly in the TSEC-listed securities, within the preliminary maximum limit of US$2.5 billion. Additionally, revision of the Securities and Exchange Law is underway to allow local securities firms to act as agents to buy and sell foreign securities, to establish overseas branches, or to become members on foreign stock exchanges. As part of its efforts to internationalise its securities industry, the Korean government plans to permit foreign securities firms to set up branch offices in Korea and form joint ventures with domestic companies. According to the Korean government's internationalisation plan, foreigners will be permitted to invest directly in Korean securities in 1992. The introduction of American Depositary Receipts (ADRs) and International Depositary Receipts (IDRs) is currently under review in Thailand. This will facilitate direct investment by international investors in Thai securities. As this trend of internationalisation continues, the degree of interdependence between the securities markets of the six DAEs and advanced markets will increase. As a result, inter-market volatility transmission will soon be a reality.

B. Impact of derivative markets on the stock market

Immediately after the market break of 1987, many individual investors who usually restricted their investment activities to the equity market complained that they were victimised by: (a) more volatile equity derivative markets; and (b) programme trading.

The question of whether trading in derivative products increases the volatility of stock returns has been examined extensively by numerous academic researchers. Many researchers, including Edwards (1988a, 1988b), Grossman (1988) and Schwert (1990), concluded that derivative markets had no significant impact on stock market volatility. Gerety and Mulherin (1990) analysed intra-day stock market volatility in the 1933-1989 period. Their findings suggest that: (a) October 1987 was indeed the most volatile month; (b) yet, that month was the exception, not the rule, in the post-1982 world of stock index futures; (c) no systematic increase in intra-day volatility after the introduction of index futures; and (d) the 1930s, a period without index futures, experienced greater volatility than did the 1982-1989 period. Becketti and Roberts (1990) estimated the frequency of jumps, which are defined as rises and falls of more than about 1.75 per cent in the Standard & Poor's (S&P) 500 composite index from July 1962 to August 1990.[5] They also found little or no relationship between stock market volatility and either the existence of or the level of activity in the stock index futures market. The Becketti and Roberts results are particularly interesting since their definition of market volatility is not the same as the traditional statistical measure of variability. Their definition represents so-called "jump" volatility that concerns legislators, regulators, and market makers more than the traditional measure of variability.

The NYSE defines programme trading as the simultaneous purchase or sale of 15 or more stocks with a total market value of at least $1 million. The NYSE member firms are required to submit daily reports on programme trades, including both principal and customer account transactions since May 1988. The consolidated reports are now available from NYSE on a weekly basis. Classified under programme trading are 17 trading strategies which include index arbitrage, portfolio insurance, and tactical asset allocation. Index arbitrage is the purchase or sale of a basket of stocks in conjunction with the sale or purchase of derivative index products. Although the price of index futures is highly correlated with the value of underlying stocks, arbitrage opportunities arise due to the price differentials between the two that are not justified by the "carrying" cost. Portfolio insurance is a strategy of selling index futures or taking long put or short call option positions when prices decline in order to ensure that the value of a portfolio does not go below some floor level. This dynamic hedging technique tends to destabilize the market. Tactical asset allocation is another method of adjusting the proportion of stocks in the portfolio over time through the buying and selling of index futures or options contracts rather than underlying stocks. The programme trading volume ranges from 8 to 11 per cent of the total NYSE trading volume. Index arbitrage remains the most important trading strategy because it usually accounts for approximately one-half of total programme trading at NYSE. Index arbitrage and portfolio insurance were seen as major villains in the market crash in October 1987.

Although the index futures market may not increase stock market volatility under normal circumstances, programme trading may exacerbate or accelerate an overall price fall in the cash market. For example, a drastic decline in the cash market may trigger futures selling by institutional investors who want to maintain a certain floor level through their strategy of portfolio insurance. This may cause the futures contract to sell at a substantial discount, which in turn triggers index arbitrage in which arbitrageurs buy the futures contracts and sell in the cash market. This may trigger another set of transactions related to portfolio insurance and index arbitrage, further depressing the cash market price.[6] Relevant for this report are two studies which examined the relationship between programme trading and intra-day market volatility. Grossman (1988) reported no significant relationship between the two from January 1987 to October 1987. Unlike Grossman, Furbush (1989) examined the impact of different strategies of programme trading -- i.e., index arbitrage, tactical asset allocation, and others -- on intra-day market volatility from October 1988 to April 1989. His findings indicate that both the total level of programme trading and the level of index arbitrage were positively correlated with intra-day volatility; the level of asset allocation was insignificantly negatively correlated with volatility; and the level of programme trading in other categories was marginally positively correlated with volatility. The inconsistency of the results may have been caused by the difference in the definition of volatility and the different study period; further investigation of the issue is warranted. Some researchers, on the other hand, advocated the positive effects of equity derivative markets on equity market. Froot, Gammill, and Perold (1990) reported that the predictability of short-term stock returns has declined markedly since 1983, contemporaneously with the growth of programme trading in the US market. This implies that equity derivative markets and programme trading played a critical role in enhancing stock market efficiency. The absence of predictability is a fundamental feature of a well-functioning market. In the winter 1987/1988 issue of *Quality of Markets Quarterly*, the ISE suggested that the limited amount of programme trading in the London market might have caused the FT-SE futures to trade at a substantial discount during the 1987 market crash rather than the reverse.

If equity derivative markets and programme trading are not the villains to be blamed for the market break of October 1987, then who was the real villain? Sato (1991) raised this question in his address delivered at the Second Annual Pacific-Basin Finance Conference held in Bangkok, Thailand, in June 1990. He suggested that the real villain was the lack of sufficient adaptations in the entire financial community to the development of derivative markets and new trading strategies. Specifically, he pointed out that the disconnection between the cash and derivative markets increased panic sentiment which caused free falls in the futures markets and later in the cash market.

Of the six DAEs, only Hong Kong and Singapore had experience in trading index futures contracts. The Hang Seng Index futures and the Nikkei Stock Average futures were introduced in Hong Kong and Singapore in May and September 1986, respectively. Since the Nikkei Stock Average futures contracts are written on 225 Japanese stocks listed under the first section of the TSE, trading of these contracts in the SIMEX had very little bearing on stock market volatility in Singapore, even though the local financial system faced systemic risks that could have resulted from the potential breakdown in clearing and settlement in Singapore during the market break of 1987. Nevertheless, the selling pressure and the surge in sell orders were handled smoothly without a single incident of default in Singapore in October 1987. Credit should be given to the government of Singapore which initiated many programmes to strengthen Singapore's financial system after its near-collapse due to the Pan-Electric Industries crisis in 1985. The Hang Seng index is computed using 33 blue chip stocks of Hong Kong. Therefore, it is valid to question the impact of the Hong Kong futures market on its cash market. Freris (1990) reported that the introduction of stock futures trading in Hong Kong had no measurable effect on stock price volatility. He further suggested that there was no concrete and quantifiable evidence of programme trading taking place in Hong Kong. This conclusion was shared by the Securities Review Committee (SRC) which released a report entitled "The Operation and Regulation of the Hong Kong Securities Industry" (1988) after the 1987 market crash. According to the SRC report, there was little evidence indicating that the Hong Kong stock market was a victim of the so-called cascade scenario in which programme trading induced a free fall in stock prices. Nevertheless, the SRC report mentioned the possibility of complete failure of the Hong Kong financial system with the default of the guarantee corporation. If the guarantee corporation had defaulted, the long arbitrageurs would have had to unwind their positions on the cash market. The estimated amount was between HK$4 billion and HK$6 billion worth of shares, which would have doubled the selling pressure of HK$4.5 billion worth of trades that eventually hit the stock market on 26th October when the SEHK resumed trading.

Chapter IV

Market mechanisms

A. Market structures

Market structures in general have two distinct systems: auction or order-driven system versus dealer or quote-driven system. Auction or order-driven markets emphasize an accurate assessment of supply and demand by requiring all orders to interact. Trading is done by brokers who simply accept buy and sell orders from investors and let the price of a security be determined by demand for and supply of that security in the marketplace. In contrast, dealer or quote-driven markets emphasize market liquidity by increasing market continuity and price stabilisation. Market continuity is achieved by minimising the time it takes for investors to trade, while price stabilisation is obtained by minimising the deviations of the market price from the intrinsic value. Market continuity and price stabilisation represent major functions of market makers. During periods of panic selling, market continuity is sacrificed for the benefit of short-term price stability or vice versa.

Two types of market makers exist in the NYSE: specialists and upstairs market makers. The upstairs market makers (registered with the NYSE as block positioners) are the block trading desks of big securities firms. Specialists in the NYSE play three roles: broker, dealer, and auctioneer. A specialist acts as a broker when other members leave limit orders that he records in his book and executes when the market price reaches the limit price. A specialist acts a dealer when he trades against the market, buys [sells] when the public is a net seller [buyer], by using his own capital. A specialist acts as an auctioneer when he sets a "fair" opening price which clears all accumulated market orders. In return for his function as a dealer, the NYSE confers a monopoly on the specialist for each stock traded on NYSE. Unlike specialists who make markets only in assigned stocks, upstairs market makers can handle any stock as long as block trades are involved. Naturally, upstairs market making is highly competitive. Market making structures in futures and options markets are different from those in equity markets. Because of the open and competitive rule, market makers (commonly known as "locals") in stock index futures markets are not required to make a fair and orderly market unlike specialists on the NYSE. Also in contrast to the stock markets, prearranged trading is prohibited; therefore, block trading, as practiced by "upstairs" block traders for NYSE stocks, is not permitted in the futures markets. Unlike the NYSE and options exchanges, there are no computerised trade execution systems on the futures exchanges. Market making practices vary among organised exchanges which trade options on stocks and stock indices. Market makers in options markets are responsible for fair and orderly markets. There are two types of members at the TSE: regular members and "saitori" members. Regular members are securities companies trading on the exchange as principals or agents with no market making obligations. Saitori members maintain a central order book for each of their "franchise" stocks allocated by the TSE and match orders in accordance with price priority and time precedence. Saitori members are neither allowed to trade any listed stock for their own account, nor can they accept orders from the investing public. Thus, the TSE market is a pure order-driven market without any help of responsible market makers. The US NASDAQ/OTC and London's International Stock Exchange (ISE) market makers must also make continuous markets but have no obligation to stabilise the prices. The Toronto Stock Exchange in Canada maintains both features of auction and dealer markets. The market maker's function co-exists with a basically order-driven automated trading system. Since the obligations of exchange members vary, the distinction between auction and dealer markets tends to be less meaningful. The TSE members act merely as brokers matching buyers and sellers, while the NYSE, NASDAQ/OTC market, and ISE have market makers acting as both brokers and dealers.

The performance of NYSE market makers during the 1987 market break was mixed. They faced three choices for handling panic-selling situations: (a) increase the spread between buying and selling prices; (b) use less of their capital to take positions; and (c) withdraw from making markets. Based on 31 stocks for which detailed trading data were available, the Presidential Task Force on Market Mechanisms (the Brady Commission) concluded that NYSE specialists performed stabilising functions on 18 and 12 stocks on 19th and 20th October, respectively, by counterbalancing market trends. For the remaining stocks, specialists either destabilized the markets or ceased performing their functions. The upstairs market makers in the NYSE also minimised their exposure. The lack of market making activity during the period of panic selling was also a common problem observed in the NASDAQ/OTC and ISE markets.

In the absence of responsible market makers, the TSE adopted two measures to maintain market continuity and short-term price fluctuations: (a) special bid or asked quotes; and (b) price limits. When there is a major order imbalance, the TSE requires that saitori members indicate a "special bid quote" or a "special asked quote," implying that a major imbalance exists between buy and sell orders. A special quote is publicly disseminated through the TSE market information system, enabling market participants to respond to the imbalance. If contra orders come into the market and equilibrium is established at the special quote, the quote is withdrawn by saitori members. If the imbalance continues, saitori members can renew the special quote upward or downward at an interval of every five minutes or more within the predetermined amount until equilibrium is reached. The TSE maintains daily price limits for individual stocks to prevent day-to-day wild swings in stock prices and also to provide a "time-out" for publicising a major price rise or decline in a stock. TSE's daily price limits are set in terms of absolute yen depending upon the price range of each stock for the purpose of simplicity. As the price limits simply prohibit bids and offers at a price beyond the limits, the market for a stock is open for trading within the limit, even after the stock hits it. The daily price limit also applies to the special quotes.

The specialist in the NYSE relies on opening delays when there is a significant imbalance of buy and sell orders before the trading begins. Similarly, when there is an imbalance of orders during the trading day beyond his control, he can request permission from a floor official to halt trading. NYSE rules require a delayed opening or trading halt to be reported on the tape. On the two critical dates of 19th and 20th October, the Brady Commission report suggested that the number and duration of opening delays and trading halts were surprisingly limited.[7] Unlike futures markets, no price limit rule applies to NYSE market making processes.

During October 1987, the Tokyo market declined by 13 per cent, while the New York, London, and Toronto markets declined by 26, 22, and 23 per cent in local currencies, respectively. Because many other factors must have affected performance in these three major markets, one cannot make any meaningful inference regarding the effectiveness of the TSE's special quote system and price limits. However, it is interesting to note Telser's (1989) suggestion that the price limit rule may be considered as an alternative to the NYSE specialist system.

Stock exchanges of all six DAEs have adopted an auction or order-driven market system. Several reasons may explain this consistent pattern. First, the role of individual investors is significant in the securities markets of the six DAEs. In contrast, the typical dealer or quote-driven markets in the NYSE, NASDAQ/OTC, and ISE markets are dominated by institutional investors. Second, the relatively low trading cost may be another consideration which dictated the securities markets of six DAEs to adopt the order-driven market system. Third, historically in any Asian society, there has been a deep-rooted distrust of "deal-making," which is typical of the dealer system. Fourth, regulatory considerations are less complicated. For the effective performance of the dealer system, regulators must pay attention to the risk exposure and capital adequacy of market makers who normally deal with large institutional investors and counterbalance the market trend. Nevertheless, as the trading volume increases and the role of institutional investors becomes more prominent in DAEs' securities markets, the need for market makers may arise. Additionally, the question of the capital adequacy of exchange member firms becomes more serious as they tend to take positions in other markets for bond and derivative securities as well as international securities markets, even if domestic equity markets remain order-driven without market intermediaries. After the 1987 market crash, the SRC reviewed the market structure for Hong Kong, but it suggested that there would be no pressing need for a dealer system similar to that existing in the NYSE, NASDAQ/OTC, and ISE markets. The following reasons were given for this recommendation: (a) no evidence indicated that the existing order-driven system failed; (b) the cost of implementing a dealer system would be considerable; (c) a dealer system might result in the monopoly of market making by a few, large international securities companies with large endowed capital; and (d) the protection of existing brokers' profit margin is needed. These reasons are not applicable only to Hong Kong, but they may be appropriate justification for other DAEs.

It is interesting to note that the dealer system was adopted for over-the-counter (OTC) markets in Korea, Singapore, and Thailand. The Korean OTC market was introduced in April 1987 to provide small and medium-size companies with fund-raising opportunities through the securities market. The OTC market complements the KSE's organised market. A total of 47 companies were registered on the OTC market with a trading volume of W 4.3 billion (US$6.3 million) or about 4 per cent of trading value of the KSE-listed securities. To be eligible for admission to the OTC market, a company must be enrolled with the Korean SEC and registered with the Korean Securities Dealers Association (KSDA) under the sponsorship of at least two securities companies. Both sponsoring and non-sponsoring securities companies may serve as market makers of the OTC securities. Market makers make trading and market information available through the KSDA. The Taiwan OTC market was established in 1982 to facilitate trading in government and corporate bonds. At present, the Taipei Securities Dealers Association (TSDA) is in charge of OTC trading in government bonds, corporate bonds, and financial debentures under the supervision of Taiwan SEC. For the first time in December 1989, the Taiwan OTC market began trading equity shares of the National Investment Trust Co., Ltd., one of four local funds management companies. Thirty-three authorised brokers are serving the Taiwan OTC market as market makers as of 1989. The OTC markets in Korea and Taiwan are structured following the US NASDAQ. In Singapore, the Stock Exchange of Singapore Dealing and Automated Quotation (SESDAQ) initially adopted the market maker system, but it was changed to an auction system shortly afterwards.

The 1987 market break taught market participants as well as market regulators one important lesson: In the face of unprecedented selling pressure, there is no perfect market structure to handle the situation. It is impossible to ascertain that one market making structure is better than the other. All major securities markets experienced significant disruption in order flow and unusually volatile price movements despite many differences in microstructure, including the degree of competitiveness in market making, capital requirements for exchange members; and dealer market versus auction market.

B. Automation of trading systems

The SEHK is currently considering the adoption of a completely automated trading system which will provide all the necessary features for automated matching, trade execution, and dissemination of company information.[8] The proposed new system is expected to be implemented once the centralised clearing system is in place. The SEHK computer network connects directly to 5 000 trading and information terminals on the trading floor and in members' offices. Buy and sell orders are input into the computer and shown on the screen; deals are generally struck by telephone. Occasionally, trading takes place from the trading floor face to face. The SEHK reports that the existing trading system handles a daily average volume of 20 000 trades without system failure. It has the capacity to process 50 000 trades a day without a significant downgrade in performance, while the largest daily volume peaked at 46 000 trades between July 1989 and June 1990.

All securities transactions are conducted on one trading floor with 11 trading posts at the KSE. Of the 11 posts, ten are assigned to the manual handling of trading while the other is for automated trading only. Each post is equipped with computer terminals for entering trading and market information. KSE employees, stationed at each post, simply serve as auctioneers, and play no role in market making. KSE member firms simply pass their clients' orders to the exchange employees at each trading post. In addition to the usual principles of auction on the basis of price, time, and customer priority, the KSE imposes a size priority on its auction process. Hence, a large order takes precedence over a small order given simultaneous bids and offers at the same price. A single opening price is determined for each trading session. Under this method, all bids and offers submitted during a ten-minute period are considered to be simultaneous. After the opening price is determined, the continuous auction process begins.

The KSE introduced the stock market automated trading system (SMATS) in March 1988 on a limited operational basis to replace the traditional manual handling of orders. By the end of June 1990, the capacity of SMATS had been expanded to handle 912 issues or 94 per cent of the total trading volume. The SMATS receives and classifies orders by issue input through system terminals installed in securities companies located across the country. It then generates a table of orders per issue on the screen of the system monitor installed at the post. Trading contracts can be performed either automatically or semi-automatically. The transaction results are automatically transmitted by the SMATS to the member firms. The SMATS also provides necessary data for market surveillance. The system now can handle more than 250 000 quotations daily. Planned augmentation will enable the system to handle as many as 1.2 million quotations per day by the end of 1994.

The stock trading unit is ten shares and the trading unit for bonds is W 100 000 (US$148.14) par value. Odd-lot orders are handled by securities companies off the trading floor. The securities companies receiving odd-lot orders are required to trade shares for their own accounts. The KSE allows two types of transaction: (a) regular-way transactions which require the settlement to be completed on the second business day following the contract day; and (b) cash transactions which require the settlement to be completed on the contract day. Stocks and equity-related debt securities such as convertible bonds and bonds with warrants are traded as regular-way transactions. Bonds except equity-related debt securities are traded as either regular-way or cash transactions.

The KLSE's open outcry system of trading was replaced by its System on Computerised Order Routing and Execution (SCORE) in November 1989. The SCORE is a semi-automated trading system because orders are routed to the KLSE's matching room to be matched by KLSE staff. All trading orders are entered at member companies' premises. Orders entered for each trading session are good for that trading session only. Orders unexecuted at the end of a trading session have to be re-entered into the system for execution. Two price matching systems are used: (a) a call market system to determine the opening and closing price of a stock for a particular trading session; and (b) a continuous market system to match orders after the opening price is determined.

In November 1988, the KLSE established a second board for smaller companies with strong growth potential to allow them access to capital markets through KLSE listing. The Malaysian government intends to dissolve the Bumiputera Stock Exchange (BSE or Pasaran Saham Bumiputera), which is an exchange set up for Bumiputera companies in 1969. According to the government plan, the eight companies listed on the BSE will be listed on the KLSE's second board.

The SES introduced a new trading system called the Central Limit Order Book (CLOB) in July 1988. This system enabled remisiers and dealers to transmit orders directly to the computer network. It replaced the previous system in which orders were channelled to the trading floor over the telephone by the central buyers of stockbroking firms. This new system without a trading floor was initially introduced on the SESDAQ, cash, buy-in, and odd-lot markets. Under this system, all orders entered directly on to a computerised central order book maintained by the SES. Matching of orders and trade reporting is fully automated. In March 1989, this system was extended to trading of the main board securities. As a result, all transactions on the SES markets were handled by the CLOB. After all Malaysian companies on the SES were delisted on 1st January 1990, the SES established an over-the-counter market known as CLOB International for trading in shares of the Malaysian companies and six Hong Kong companies. The number of Hong Kong companies has since increased to 12 and a Philippine company has been listed. Trading on CLOB International is done through the existing CLOB system in operation for shares of Singapore companies.

The TSEC classifies all listed companies into Categories A, B, and C by their capital size, profitability, capital structure, and the status of share distribution. The minimum capital requirement is NT$400 million (US$15.28 million) for Category A, NT$200 million (US$7.64 million) for Category B, and NT$100 million (US$3.82 million) for Category C, respectively. Three types of transaction are allowed at the TSEC market: (a) regular transactions requiring settlement with the TSEC on t+2 after the day of transaction; (b) cash transactions requiring settlement on the same day of the transaction; and (c) special transactions requiring settlement on a specified day after the day of transaction. The TSEC adopted its Computer-Assisted Trading System (CATS) in August 1985 to handle initially 43 Category B stocks. Beginning in September 1988, all the listed stocks were traded through CATS. In addition to the general trading system, CATS has been expanded to include a number of sub-systems such as odd-lot transactions, full-delivery transactions, block trading, convertible bonds transactions, and market information systems. To determine the opening price and subsequent prices, the same type of pricing principles as discussed for Korea and Malaysia is applied. The CATS is semi-automated in the sense that matching of buy and sell quotes is executed by the matching staff in the TSEC matching room, while data transmission, data summaries, and file updates are performed by CATS. Market orders have been prohibited by the SEC since October 1987, and currently only limit orders are allowed. According to a seven-year computerisation plan, the TSEC system expects to connect 3,900 trading terminals, with a trading capacity of 2.3 million trades and a trading value of NT$420 billion

(US$16.05 billion) per day in 1995. Compare this increased capacity with the largest number of daily stock trades recorded in 1989 which was 552 930 with a trading value of NT$192 billion (US$7.34 billion).

Trading is conducted on three separate boards at the SET: (a) main board; (b) special board; and (c) alien board. Regular trading is conducted on the main board. The minimum and maximum units under regular trading are 1 and 20 "board lots" for a single trade. The value of one "board lot" is approximately equal to B 10 000 (US$4 000), comprised of 25, 50, 100, 200, 1 000, or 2 000 shares depending on the market price of an issue. The special board trades odd lots, special lots, and big lots. An odd lot represents an order for less than one board lot number of shares, while a special lot is an order for a number of shares greater than one board lot, but not a whole number of board lots. A big lot is an order with a value exceeding B 10 million (US$0.40 million) or with a value of 10 per cent or more of the paid-up capital, whichever is smaller. The alien board is for shares that are registered to foreign owners. The minimum size deal on the foreign board is 10 board lots, but there is no limit on the maximum size of deals.

To support the expansion of trading volume, the SET is installing its new trading system called the Automated System Stock Exchange of Thailand (ASSET), which is expected to be in operation by the middle of 1991. The main features of the ASSET are: (a) automated order matching; (b) maintenance of a "public" order book; (c) calculation of market statistics; (d) support of market surveillance and regulation functions; and (e) provision of end-of-day processing. In addition, the ASSET provides facilities for negotiated trading via "advertisement of interest" and deal entry functions.[9,10] Under the ASSET, transactions are conducted through either automated order-matching deals or put-through deals. Put-through deals are achieved by either internally "crossing" two orders from the same broker or by negotiation between different brokers outside the system. The SET must approve the deal before it is considered "done," but put-through deals will not be counted as "last sales" and will not change the last deal price.

All six DAEs have been expanding the capacity of their securities markets through an automated trading system. Automation of securities markets would bring both benefits and costs. An automated system enhances market efficiency through timely dissemination of relevant information; strengthens international competitiveness through a better operating efficiency; improves market surveillance by alerting the organised exchanges and regulatory bodies of any unusual movements in securities prices; and increases trading volume through computerised order-routing, matching, price determination, and clearing and settlement. After having compared three automated trading systems (including the Chicago Mercantile Exchange's Globex system for futures, the Chicago Board Options Exchange's Retail Automated Exchange System (RAES) for options, and the US NASDAQ's Small Order Execution System (SOES)) with the traditional floor trading, Domowitz (1990) reported that the automated systems performed better than floor trading in terms of price discovery, quantity determination, and total customer surplus. However, Domowitz found that customer surplus is achieved at the expense of market makers who lose between approximately 6 to 9 per cent of average trading prices when dealing on the systems rather than on the trading floor. His findings confirm the belief that the automated trading system benefits customers. Unfortunately, the magnitude of systemic risks also increases exponentially with enhanced trading volume and operating efficiency. Hence, regulatory complications must be carefully evaluated to ensure that the management of systemic risks can be maintained with minimal regulatory gaps.[11]

C. Circuit breakers

Many forms of circuit breaker have been used in various markets to stop prices from falling in times of panic selling by providing a short cooling-down period. Trading halts, price limits, and contingent restrictions on certain types of order are common examples of circuit breakers. Trading halts are temporary suspensions of trading. Price limits define upper and lower price bounds outside which trading cannot take place. Some examples of contingent restrictions are: (a) uptick rules on short sales; (b) index arbitrage "collar"; and (c) sidecar procedures. The uptick rule requires that short sales of individual stocks are allowed only after a plus or zero-plus tick. Between January and October 1988, the NYSE experimented with an index arbitrage "collar." Whenever the DJIA moved 75 points (later changed to 50 points) above or below the previous day's closing level, member firms were not to use the NYSE Designated Order Turnaround System (DOT). The DOT is an electronic order-routing system which enables member firms to transmit market and limit orders in all NYSE-listed securities directly to the specialist post or to the member firm's booth. The sidecar procedures kick in when the S&P 500 futures contract declines 12 points from the previous day's close. Under the procedure, the execution of DOT-submitted programme trades is delayed at least five minutes. Additionally, limits on block trades, stock market stabilisation fund, and margin regulations are discussed.

One of five major recommendations made by the Brady Commission was related to circuit breakers. The Brady Commission recommended that circuit breaker mechanisms should be formulated and implemented to protect the market system. The Smith Panel also recommended that: co-ordinated circuit breakers be introduced to halt or limit trading in times of market stress; these measures should be mandatory across all domestic equity and equity derivative markets; and enhanced price and trade information should be made available during times when circuit breakers are triggered. Proponents argue that circuit breakers are beneficial because: (a) they may reduce market volatility; (b) they may reduce credit risk by providing time for intra-day margin calls to be made and for margin payments to be collected; (c) they may correct the order imbalance; and (d) they may help restore individual investor confidence. The US SEC's Report on *Trading Analysis of October 13 and 16, 1989* (May 1990) supported this view based on trading activities in the recent market break experienced in October 1989. According to the SEC Report, the imposition of the CME's 12-point price limit for the S&P futures coincided with a sharp drop-off in the level of programme selling on the NYSE and a reduction in the rate of the price decline in NYSE stocks. After the price limit expired, the rate of the price decline in NYSE stocks increased substantially. Many studies, however, cast doubt on the effectiveness of circuit breakers in reducing market volatility and correcting a large imbalance between supply of and demand for stocks. For example, the US CFTC's *Report on Stock Index Futures and Cash Market Activity During October 1989* (May 1990) suggested that: (a) the 12-point shock absorber did not appear to have moderated intra-day market volatility on 13th October 1989; (b) when the 12-point price limit was replaced by a 30-point limit on the S&P futures market, a significant increase in the overall volatility of the underlying S&P 500 stocks was noted; and (c) the expiration of the 12-point futures price limit was associated with a decrease in stock market volatility. Numerous examples are also cited by the opponents of circuit breaker mechanisms. First, a de facto circuit breaker provided by the weekend closing between 4 p.m., Friday, 16th October 1987, and 9:30 a.m., Monday, 19th October did nothing to prevent the market crash. Second, Amihud and Mendelson (1987) and Stoll and Whaley (1990) documented empirical evidence that the open-to-open market volatility is higher than the close-to-close volatility. The opening of trade occurs after a de facto circuit breaker that lasts from the close of trade the previous day to the opening of trade in the morning. This implies that the process of halting trade to collect orders overnight does not reduce volatility. Third, the Hong Kong market was closed for one week following the market break. When trading resumed on 26th October the market declined more than 30 per cent. The positive role of circuit breaker mechanisms in reducing market volatility was not realised. Fama (1989) stressed that trading halts simply delay the adjustment of prices to changes in fundamental values. He further suggested that empirical evidence reported by Roll (1989) is consistent with this view because the 1987 market crash was as strong in markets that imposed trading halts on or around 19th October as in those that did not. Even if circuit breakers reduce volatility, it is not clear whether the benefits exceed the cost associated with the illiquidity and inefficiency which might result.

1. Trading halts

In the United States, the SEC and stock exchanges are authorised to enforce trading halts. Trading halts at the NYSE are usually imposed on the basis of: (a) a substantial imbalance of buy or sell orders; or (b) a significant news announcement. The first type of halt is initiated by specialists, whereas the second type is initiated by the listed company, the exchange, or specialists. The SEC initiates trading halts in any or all securities when it suspects violation of securities laws. In general, NYSE-initiated halts (which occur about three times a day) are designed to reduce the specialist's market-making risk exposure, while SEC-initiated halts (which average about 80 per year) are regulatory actions intended to protect investors. Hopewell and Schwartz (1976), who examined about 1 000 trading halts enforced by the NYSE in 1974 and 1975, reported the presence of pre-suspension anticipatory price movement, price adjustment during the suspension period, and complete price adjustment after the suspension. This observation is significant since it implies that trading halts led to the recovery of normal market equilibrium for the security suspended. Howe and Schlarbaum (1986) reported substantial price devaluations of the suspended securities during and after the suspension period. Kabir (1991) has examined 1 902 trading halts enforced by the London Stock Exchange between January 1971 and March 1988. He also reports the presence of anticipatory price behaviour and significant positive abnormal returns following trading halts. This implies that either the complete impact of information release takes place gradually, or not all relevant information is disclosed during the suspension period.

Stock exchanges of the six DAEs impose trading halts if any circumstances exist that may result in other than the "fair and orderly" trading of listed securities. Hence, trading halts in the six DAEs are very similar to exchange-initiated suspensions at the NYSE.

2. Price limits

Although price limits are prevalent in the US futures market, no daily fluctuation limits are imposed in the stock market. The major argument in favour of price limits is that excessive price movements are caused by irrational speculation and can be cooled down through price limits. For example, the *TSE 1990 Fact Book* says:

> "...the TSE maintains price limits to prevent day-to-day wild swings in stock prices and also to provide a time-out ...for resultant evaluation of the situation by the investing public."

However, there are numerous arguments against price limits. First, if new information requires a price change larger than the allowable price range, trading halts will delay the determination of equilibrium prices. Second, price limits lock traders out and in when trading is most needed. Third, if market participants know that trading will be stopped when prices reach a certain level, price limits may have a "magnet effect." As prices approach the limit, traders may buy or sell frantically before the circuit breaker is triggered, accelerating the process. Usually, price limits last for a predetermined period of time, ranging from a few minutes to several hours. Daily price limits specify a maximum price change for the whole day and, once triggered, remain in effect until the next day's opening. A recent study by Ma, Rao, and Sears (1989) provides an interesting insight into the relationship between price limits and price volatility. This study examined the behaviour of futures prices for a selected group of commodities including corn, soybeans, silver, and Treasury bonds before and after daily price limits were hit. This study's empirical evidence indicates that prices tend to stabilize or reverse directions following the limit moves and further that volatility tends to drop off substantially when trading resumes, thus suggesting that (a) price limits may provide a cooling period for the futures market and (b) market liquidity may not be severely impaired by the limit move process.

Table I summarises price limits in the securities markets of the six DAEs. No price limits are imposed in the Hong Kong and Singapore markets. The KSE has established the daily price change limits based on the previous day's closing price. Price limits are applicable to equity and equity-related debt securities and vary according to price levels. In terms of percentage, price limits in Korea range from 2 to 6.67 per cent.[12,13] The KSE has established separate daily price change limits for administrative issues. Any issue falling under the delisting criteria may be designated by the KSE as an administrative issue to warn the investing public of its exposure to excessive risk.

Table I. Price limits (As of December 1989)

Hong Kong   No price limits

Korea	Previous day's closing price		Price limits	Percentage limits
Below	W 3 000		100	- 3.33%
	W 3 000	- 4 990	200	6.67% - 4.01%
	5 000	- 6 990	300	6.00% - 4.29%
	7 000	- 9 990	400	5.71% - 4.00%
	10 000	- 14 900	600	6.00% - 4.03%
	15 000	- 19 900	800	5.33% - 4.02%
	20 000	- 29 900	1 000	5.00% - 3.34%
	30 000	- 39 900	1 300	4.33% - 2.61%
	40 000	- 49 900	1 600	4.00% - 3.21%
	50 000	- 69 900	2 000	4.00% - 2.86%
	70 000	- 99 900	2 500	3.57% - 2.50%
	100 000	- 149 900	3 000	3.00% - 2.00%
	150 000	or more	4 000	2.67% -

Malaysia   30 per cent of previous day's closing price

Singapore   No price limits

Taiwan   7 per cent of previous day's closing price

Thailand   10 per cent of previous day's closing price

Price limits for administrative issues are much narrower than normal. In Malaysia, Taiwan, and Thailand, the daily price movements of stocks are restricted to 30 per cent, 7 per cent, and 10 per cent of the previous day's closing price, respectively. The impact of price limits on market volatility has yet to be investigated. Chung (1990) examined whether or not price limits dampen the relationship between market volatility and trading volume over time using the Korean data. The Korean data provides an interesting case because the increasing average price level effectively lowered the percentage of price limits over time. Due to the limitation of the model employed, however, no clear evidence was produced.

3. Uptick rules on short sale

Although present restrictions on short sale have been in existence in the US equity market since 1938, there are no uptick rules in London. In July 1990, the US SEC approved amendments to the NYSE Rule 80A on a one-year pilot basis. The amendment introduced an index arbitrage tick test (commonly known as "Rule 80A") which became effective in August 1990. Under Rule 80A, when the DJIA index moves 50 points or more from the previous day's close, index arbitrage orders in component stocks of the S&P 500 stock price index are subject to a tick test. In down markets sell orders may only be executed on a plus or zero-plus tick; in up markets buy orders may only be executed on a minus or zero-minus tick. The NYSE Report (1991) on Rule 80A summarised that: (a) Rule 80A reduced sell index arbitrage value per minute by 23 per cent and buy index arbitrage value per minute by 62 per cent when it was triggered on the down side and up side, respectively; (b) Rule 80A does not appear to cause serious "decoupling" of the cash and futures markets; (c) no significant "magnet effect" was observed; and (d) evidence on short-term (minute-by-minute) volatility is mixed.

Although the reported results are encouraging from the regulatory viewpoint, further examination is warranted to confirm the conclusions because of the limited number of observations and the short study period. The analysis was conducted based on 23 instances from August to December 1990.[14] McMillan and Overdahl (1991) examined the impact of Rule 80A on volatility, market linkage, and costs of trading. Their findings are: (a) cash market volatility of minute returns was lower after the implementation of Rule 80A, but futures price volatility is unaffected; (b) Rule 80A weakened, but did not eliminate the linkage between cash and futures markets; and (c) trading costs in the cash market, as measured by the average bid-asked spread for S&P 500 stocks, declined by a small amount following the triggering of Rule 80A, while trading costs in the futures markets increased. Their results corroborate those in the NYSE Report (1991). In his keynote address at the Second Annual Pacific-Basin Finance Conference held in Bangkok, Thailand, in June 1990, Miller (1990) emphasized that the Smith Panel broke with the Brady Commission in one important respect. The Brady Commission noted that the most chaotic market conditions during the market break in October 1987 had occurred when the futures market and the cash market had become disconnected. The Smith Panel, by endorsing Rule 80A, had voted, in effect, to disconnect the markets by severing the arbitrage link between the two markets.

4. Index arbitrage "collar"

Between January and October 1988, the NYSE introduced an index arbitrage "collar" designed to reduce the volume of index arbitrage. The idea was simple. Whenever the DJIA moved 75 points (later changed to 50 points) above or below the previous day's closing average, NYSE members firms were not to use the DOT automated order routing system. Index arbitrage was not impossible because it could be done as orders were transmitted manually. However, this restriction increased the transaction costs of index arbitrage and lengthened order execution time. Mann and Sofianos (1990) reported that the increased cost of index arbitrage appeared to reduce the cash market volatility of one-minute returns, but not the volatility of one-hour returns. The "collar" restriction was eventually abandoned and was replaced by the circuit breaker system which was co-ordinated with the CME at the recommendation of the Brady Commission.

Despite the recommendation for co-ordinated circuit breakers by the NYSE Market Volatility and Investor Confidence Panel, circuit breakers adopted by the NYSE and the CME are not co-ordinated. At the CME, the most popular stock index futures contracts, the S&P 500 futures, are traded. The S&P 500 futures has an opening price limit that is five points above or below the previous day's closing price. The S&P 500 futures also has a maximum daily limit of 50 points above or below the previous day's closing price. Counterparts for neither of these circuit breakers exist on the NYSE. Some of the CME circuit breakers do have counterparts on the NYSE, but the counterparts do not always impose the same restrictions. For example, if the S&P 500 futures price falls 12 points from the previous day's close, such a decline would trip circuit breakers in both the futures and stock markets. The circuit breaker in the futures market keeps the S&P 500 futures price from falling further for 30 minutes or until 2:30 p.m., whichever comes first. The circuit breaker on the NYSE, however, only delays for five minutes programme trading orders for S&P 500 stocks entered through the NYSE DOT system.[15]

The SRC strongly recommended that the SEHK and HKFE markets be linked through co-ordinated responses to disorderly trading. No specific proposals, however, were included in the report.

5. "Sidecar" procedures

The NYSE has established "sidecar" procedures which are triggered when the price of the S&P 500 futures falls 12 points. When this 12-point limit is reached, the CME will notify the NYSE, which then puts the sidecar procedures into effect. The sidecar rule requires that market orders involving programme trading in each of the stocks underlying the S&P 500 entered into the NYSE's DOT system be routed into a separate file ("sidecar" file) for each of the stocks. After five minutes in the sidecar file, buy and sell orders are paired, and the order imbalances are reported to the specialists for the stocks. At this point, the stocks are eligible for execution.

D. Limits on block trade

Trading by large institutions accounts for almost 80 per cent of the trading volume on the NYSE, and block trade (in excess of 10 000 shares) represents about one-half of the NYSE volume. Approximately one-quarter of institutional trading is conducted in the form of programme trading. At the NYSE market, block trades occur "upstairs," off the trading floor. As the securities markets become more and more institutionalised, the specialist's role is decreasing. At the same time, there is strong resentment toward the domination of the US markets by a small number of institutions with respect to demand for and supply of securities. As a result, support for limits on block trades has been advocated in the US market. However, special arrangements for trading are noted at the securities markets of the six DAEs. For example, to facilitate block trading without causing a substantial price change in an issue, the KSE established special rules that are applicable to block sale but not purchase. The minimum size of an order for block trading is 100 000 shares, and the offer price must be lower than the existing best offer. The block trading procedure is not taken until the opening price of an issue is determined. If a member firm wants to handle its block order publicly, the KSE releases the terms of orders to the public. A member firm having a counter-bid equal to one-half or more of the number of the offered shares is not allowed to submit an order for ten minutes after the block order is released. The TSEC's unit of trading, or board lot, is 1 000 shares. Block trading is used with trading amounts of 500 units or more, or with a par value in excess NT$5 million (US$0.19 million). Buying and selling orders are submitted to the TSEC between 2 and 3:30 p.m. The bid and offer prices are restricted to the closing price of that morning's trading session.[16]

E. Stock market stabilisation fund

The Korean and Thai governments employed an indirect method of market intervention by setting up stock market stabilisation funds with contributions from securities companies, insurance companies, banks, institutional investors, and listed companies. The main purpose of these funds was to slow the rapid decline in stock prices. The Korean stock market stabilisation fund was established in May 1990 with the contributed fund of W 4 trillion (US$5.92 billion) or approximately 4 per cent of Korea's total market capitalisation. A similar fund, called the Ruam Pattana II Fund, was established by 35 member brokers, sub-brokers, the Industrial Finance Corporation of Thailand and the Stock Exchange of Thailand. This is a closed-end fund with total capital of B 5 billion (US$198.57 million) or about one per cent of total market capitalisation. Although the effectiveness of this type of indirect market intervention has yet to be examined carefully, market participants are ambivalent about this type of market stabilisation measures.

Korea introduced another measure called the Guarantee Stock Fund in September 1990 which guarantees a ten per cent minimum annual return to its investors. The fund was established with a total of W 2.6 trillion (US$3.85 billion) contributed by investment trust companies. Although it increases market liquidity and the role of institutional investors in the Korean securities markets, losses to be incurred by participating investment trust companies may far exceed any benefits from the operation of this fund.

F. Margin regulations

Since the market crash of October 1987, considerable attention has been refocused on the adequacy and consistency of margin regulations in the US markets for common stocks, stock index futures, stock options, stock index options, and stock index futures options. Additionally, the effectiveness of margin regulations in curbing speculative activities gained new importance among regulators and market participants. The US Congress first introduced official margin regulations on stock transactions in 1934 with the belief that margin requirements would discourage highly leveraged investors from engaging in excessively speculative activities by directly restricting the amount of extendable credit. The Federal Reserve Board set the initial margin requirement at 50 per cent of the market value when buying stock on margin or selling stock short, but has not exercised its authority to regulate the maintenance margin level. Individual stock exchanges and the National Association of Securities Dealers (NASD) are allowed to establish a maintenance margin. The NYSE maintenance margin levels are 25 per cent for long stocks, 30 per cent for short stocks, and 10 per cent for long stocks that are offset by shorts in the same security.[17] If the stock price rises after the initial purchase, the investor can withdraw the differential from his margin account or can use it to buy additional stock. If the price declines and his equity position falls below the so-called predetermined maintenance margin, the investor is required to add funds to his margin account. The Federal Reserve Board changed the initial margin requirements 22 times between 1935 and 1974. These requirements have remained unchanged since 1974, which indicates that the Federal Reserve Board has suspended the use of margin requirements as a policy tool for controlling speculative activities and market volatility.[18]

Margin regulation in Japan is similar to that in the United States. Initial margin requirements are fulfilled by either cash or securities. Since September 1990, the initial margin requirement has been set at 30 per cent. When securities are used as collateral in lieu of cash, the so-called "loan value" of securities is lower than the value of the securities themselves. There are predetermined loan value rates applicable to different types of securities for haircut: 80 per cent for stocks, 95 per cent for government bonds, 90 per cent for government-guaranteed bonds, 85 per cent for other bonds, and 80 per cent for convertible bonds. Although the initial margin requirements and loan value rates have changed many times, the maintenance margin has remained at 20 per cent of the stock price at the time it was originally bought or sold on margin. Additionally, interest rates for margin transactions fluctuate with the Bank of Japan's official discount rate. The buyer on margin pays an interest to the security firm at a rate usually equivalent to the discount rate plus 3.25 per cent for the period of time until the loan is repaid. The short seller of borrowed securities receives interest at a rate usually equivalent to the discount rate minus 1.25 per cent. The TSE has been changing margin requirements and loan value rates frequently to control market volatility. For example, there have been 14 and 12 changes in the initial margin requirements and loan value rates, respectively, since October 1987.

Earlier studies examined the relationship between margin requirements and the level of the market.[19] Their findings provide little support for the hypothesised negative relationship. A recent study by Hardouvelis and Peristiani (1989) reported that: (a) the increase in margin requirements that followed a period of rising stock prices reduced the level of the market; and (b) the effect of margin decrease was nevertheless ambiguous because the decrease did not occur until after the market rebounded substantially. Thus, it is not clear whether the margin decrease further pushed up the price level or the market simply followed its own upward momentum. The same study reports that the change in margin requirements in Japan was followed by an immediate reversal of the price level. More recent studies have focused on the relationship between margin requirements and market volatility. Weak empirical evidence on the negative relationship between margin requirements and stock price volatility has been reported for the US market by Ferris and Chance (1988) and Hsieh and Miller (1990). Using the US data, Salinger (1989) observed that margin debt was not primarily associated with downside volatility and margin requirements were not associated with upside volatility. Thus, he concluded that stock price volatility was driven by some other factor. Schwert (1989) also cast doubt about the efficacy of margin regulations as a policy tool to curb stock price volatility. In contrast, empirical evidence on the Japanese market shows that an increase in margin requirements reduces daily volatility and, conversely, a decrease in margin requirements increases daily volatility.[20] Regarding the association between margin requirements in the *futures* markets and stock market volatility, Kupiec (1990) found a positive relationship — that is, high margin rates in the futures markets tend to be associated with periods of above-average volatility in the cash market. Kupiec attributed his finding to prudent management of the futures margin.

Of the six DAEs included in this report, only three countries, including Korea, Taiwan, and Thailand, use margin regulations extensively. Singapore and Malaysia only recently introduced margin requirements into their securities markets to increase market liquidity rather than control market volatility. No established rules on short sales exist in Singapore. The SEHK is currently considering introduction of margin regulations even though margin trading has been in existence in an unstructured manner in the past.

Only Korea and Taiwan report summary statistics of margin trading. In 1989, total margin transactions in Korea amounted to 778.4 million shares or 23 per cent of the total trading volume. Only one-quarter of total margin transactions were represented by short sales, with the remainder represented by margin purchase. The TSEC reported that the total number of margin transactions was 11.2 billion shares or 5 per cent of the total TSEC trading volume. Short sales accounted for about 9 per cent of total margin transactions. In Japan, margin trading accounted for 16 per cent of the total trading volume in the same year.

Korean securities companies may extend credit to their customers by using their own money or stocks, or by borrowing from the Korea Securities Finance Corporation (KSFC). The former is called "Brokers' Self Credit," and the latter is known as

"KSFC Margin Loans." Korean securities are classified into a margin group and a non-margin group. Margin stocks consist of all the first section securities except those issued by brokerage firms and corporations having capital stock of less than one billion won. The SEC, given jurisdiction over the appropriate level of margin requirements, has changed the official margin requirement 18 times since 1977. The margin requirement typically ranges from 40 to 100 per cent. Ten out of the 18 changes have been made since October 1987. The initial margin requirement is currently 40 per cent for both margin buyers and short sellers. The loan value rate is determined by the KSE: 70 per cent for stocks, 90 per cent for government securities and government-guaranteed bonds, and 80 per cent for corporate-issued debentures. The maintenance margin has remained unchanged at 130 per cent of the investor's equity. In addition to the initial and maintenance margin, the KSE requires that a good-faith deposit be made when an order is placed with a member firm. In cash transactions, the cash needed for purchases or the securities to be offered for sale must be deposited at the time an order is placed. For regular-way transactions, cash for purchases and cash or securities for sales must be collected as a good-faith deposit. The minimum deposit rate, usually ranging from 40 to 100 per cent, is set by the KSE. The current rate is 40 per cent. However, institutional investors may be exempted from this requirement. In the Korean market, changes in the both initial margin requirements and good-faith deposits have been used extensively to stimulate or cool down the market. However, Ahn (1991) raises doubt about the effectiveness of both margin regulations and good-faith deposits as a policy tool based on the experience in the Korean market between 1980 and 1989[21]. Margin loans or stock loans must be covered not later than 150 days subsequent to the date of margin transaction.

The Korean SEC sets the credit ceiling to curb excessive margin transactions. The margin-buying position in a single issue may not exceed 20 per cent of its listed shares, while the position of short sales in a single issue may not exceed 10 per cent of its listed shares. Securities companies may not extend margin loans in excess of its shareholders' equity. For short sales, the maximum is 50 per cent of the shareholders' equity. A securities company may extend up to a W 50 million (US$74 000) margin loan to a single customer and up to W 20 million (US$30 000) margin loan in the case of a stock loan. Margin transactions in 1989 totaled 778 million shares, which accounted for slightly more than 33 per cent of the total trading volume of margin stocks.

The margin system for stock transactions was introduced in Taiwan in April 1974. In the initial stage, the Bank of Taiwan, the Bank of Communications, and the Land Bank of Taiwan were authorised to loan money for margin transactions. The Fuh-Hwa Securities Finance Company (FHSFC), established as the only accredited securities financial institution in April 1980, took over all the securities financing business. FHSFC further began to engage in lending securities to investors beginning in July 1980. An investor who wants to start margin transactions must first open an account with a broker who then can apply for him at FHSFC to open a margin account. When a transaction is made under the margin system, the investor must deposit a certain percentage of the trading value with FHSFC as the margin requirement. The shares purchased or the proceeds received on a margin transaction become the collateral for the unpaid balance.

Listed stocks that are eligible for margin transactions are subject to "Eligibility Criteria for Margin Trading Stocks." The settlement of purchase and sales made in margin accounts is the same as that for any normal market transactions. The number of stocks which were authorised for margin transaction was 129, an increase of 25 from 1988.

The SET is authorised to control initial margin requirements in Thailand and has changed the margin requirements 20 times since April 1977. Fourteen out of 20 changes were made after the market crash of October 1987. However, the maintenance margin remained unchanged at 40 per cent. The margin payment must be made in cash, and securities are not allowed to substitute for cash.

The Securities Review Committee recommended that margin regulations be promulgated in Hong Kong and margin trading in each stock be published regularly. Short selling is currently prohibited in Hong Kong. The SFC has been reviewing the possibility of introducing arrangements for short selling to increase market liquidity. Stock borrowing and lending have been under review by the SFC and SEHK to facilitate the Hong Kong settlement system as well as short selling. Although no written information is publicly available from SFC or SEHK, the two organisations are preparing draft margin regulations for internal review.

Margin regulation in Singapore has been in place when the 1986 Securities Industry Act 1986 and Regulations came into effect. The margin deposited by a customer with an SES-member firm may be in the form of cash, securities issued by the government and its agencies, margin securities, and other instruments approved by SES. The required initial margin is at least 150 per cent of the "debit balance" in the margin account. The debit balance means the cash amount owed by a customer in his margin account before deducting cash deposited by him as margin. Whenever the "equity" in the margin account (which is the sum of margin and current market value of securities purchased on margin) falls below 140 per cent of the debit balance, a margin call is made to bring the equity to no less than the stipulated 140 per cent. If the customer's equity falls below 130 per cent of the debit balance, the member firm has absolute discretion to liquidate the margin account, including margin securities deposited, to maintain the 140 per cent margin level. No explicit rules exist on short sales in Singapore. Both initial and maintenance margin requirements have not been changed since 1986, which implies that margin regulations are not considered by SES as a policy tool to control the amount of credit available in the market.

Margin transactions represent one of the recent developments adopted by the KLSE. A set of new rules on financing the purchase of securities on margin accounts was introduced in November 1989. The KLSE margin rules are almost identical to those adopted by the SES with the one exception that both initial and maintenance margins are set at 150 per cent of the debit balance in the margin account. Since their first introduction, margin requirements have not been changed.

Chapter V

Clearing and settlement systems

Various international organisations initiated efforts to identify problems and issues related to clearing and settlement systems and to formulate solutions. The studies conducted by these organisations may be classified into three categories depending on their major focus. Category I emphasizes clearing and settlement systems at a national equity market. A report entitled "Clearance and Settlement Systems in the World's Securities Markets" commissioned by the Group of Thirty (G 30) belongs to Category I. Category II emphasizes cross-border clearing and settlement systems. Three major studies/reports are: a European Economic Community (EEC) report entitled *Study on Improvements in the Settlement of Cross-Border Securities Transactions in the European Economic Community* (July 1988), an FIBV study entitled *Improving International Settlements* (June 1989), and an International Society of Securities Administrators (ISSA) *Symposium Report* (May 1988). Category III focuses on clearing and settlement systems in derivative securities markets. A study by Kessler, entitled *Risks in the Clearing and Settlement Systems of Markets for Financial Futures and Options* (forthcoming, 1992) may be classified under this category. Additionally, the Brady Commission Report and the SRC Report on the Hong Kong market discussed this issue extensively.

In the context of this study, two reports by G-30 and FIBV would be most relevant since they provide a useful framework for assessing the current status and future internationalisation of the clearing and settlement systems of equity markets in the six DAEs. The G-30 report recognises that while development of a single global clearing facility is not practical, agreement on a set of practices and standards is desirable. Hence, the G-30 made nine recommendations for improving the systems on a national level.

Recommendation 1:   By 1990, all comparisons of trades between direct market participants should be accomplished by t+1.

Recommendation 2:   By 1992, indirect market participants should be members of a trade comparison system.

Recommendation 3:   By 1992, each country should have a central depository function in place.

Recommendation 4:   Each country should study whether a trade netting system would be beneficial and, if so, implement it by 1992.

Recommendation 5:   Delivery versus payment (DVP) should be employed as the method for settling all securities transactions and should be in place by 1992.

Recommendation 6:   All securities administration and settlement payments should be made consistent across all instruments and markets by adopting the "Same Day Funds" convention.

Recommendation 7:   A "Rolling Settlement" system should be adopted by all markets. Final settlement should occur on t+5 by 1990 at the latest and on t+3 by 1992.

Recommendation 8:   Securities lending and borrowing should be encouraged to facilitate settlements. Any existing legal and taxation barriers should be removed by 1990.

Recommendation 9:   By 1992, each country should adopt the standard for securities messages developed by the International Organisation for Standardisation (ISO Standard 7775) and the system for securities issues as defined in the ISO Standard 6166, at least for cross-border transactions.

The task force appointed by FIBV made four recommendations for improved cross-border settlement in the future: (a) adoption of international settlement conventions as proposed by the G-30, ISSA, and EEC; (b) establishment of cross-border settlement links among national and international central securities depositories; (c) immobilisation of securities in the issuer's country and transfer by a book-entry system; (d) listing of foreign securities in their original form.

The National Securities Clearing Corporation (NSCC) handles clearing and settlement of trades in the NYSE, the American Stock Exchange, some regional exchanges, and OTC stocks[22]. The depository function is provided by the Depository Trust Company (DTC). The NSCC maintains the Clearing Fund contributed by about 400 participants. The amount of contribution by each member is determined by its settlement activity. If a participant fails to meet its obligations to the NSCC, the NSCC would: (a) liquidate the participant's position by purchasing securities to cover a failed delivery obligation or by selling securities received for a payment failure; (b) have access to the defaulting participant's deposit in the Clearing Fund; and (c) call for a larger contribution from non-defaulting participants to cover the loss and replenish the fund to the pre-default level.

There is no magic formula to determine an optimum amount of the guarantee fund as described above. A number of factors that may affect the size of the guarantee fund are: (a) daily market turnover; (b) market volatility; (c) settlement period; (d) settlement (or capital) risk; and (e) market (or position) risk. The last two factors, settlement risk and market risk, represent two major types of risk faced by a clearing corporation. Settlement risk arises when a participant fails to meet his obligations for either delivering securities or making a required payment. The clearing corporation is exposed to market risk when buying and selling the defaulting member's securities. The deviation of market price at the time of liquidation from the original contract price may represent potential losses.

Leung (1991) classifies eleven Pacific-Basin countries (including six DAEs) into three groups depending upon the stages of development. According to her classification, four of the six DAEs (Korea, Singapore, Taiwan, and Thailand) are at the mature stage, whereas Hong Kong and Malaysia have yet to make further developments to improve their clearing and settlement systems:

Introductory stage: Indonesia and Philippines.

Developmental stage: Hong Kong, Australia, New Zealand, and Malaysia.

Mature stage: Japan, Korea, Singapore, Taiwan, and Thailand.

The current Hong Kong system relies on physical settlement of individual trades. No part of the process is centralised or automated, and there is no netting of trades between brokers before settlement. At present, Hong Kong is the only country which relies on a one-sided matching (or comparison) system, while the remaining five DAEs rely on a two-sided matching system. Each selling broker is responsible for reporting a transaction within 15 minuets after the conclusion of the transaction. Any discrepancy should be reported to the SEHK no later than the end of the next trading day. Each trade must be settled by 3:45 p.m. on the day after the trade by the physical delivery of a certificate and a stamped transfer form against a cheque which, in many cases, can only be cleared a few days later. Under the current rules, registrars have 21 days to register transfers and issue new stock certificates. Shares cannot be sold pending registration because of the 24-hour settlement rule, the prohibition on short selling, and the lack of formal structure for stock lending. Recognising the inefficiency and the lack of security in the system resulting from manual handling of clearing and settlement of trades, the HKSCC was established in May 1989 and is expected to be in operation by the end of 1991. According to the proposed clearing and settlement system under review, a central securities depository will be in place, utilising an immobilisation approach which requires legislative changes to make it operational. The new settlement period proposed is t+2. A guarantee fund will be set up in the amount of HK$150 million or approximately 12 per cent of the daily trading volume at the SEHK market. Two-thirds of the fund will come from broker contributions and the remaining one-third will be made up of insurance coverage. The HKSCC plans to provide a centralised stock lending and borrowing service to participating brokers.

With the introduction of the book-entry clearing system in 1974, the KSE set up the Korea Securities Settlement Corporation (KSSC), a wholly owned subsidiary, to act as a clearing agent for KSE and the central depository. The KSE, having responsibility for the settlement of transactions, outlines the method, time, and other matters related to the settlement. The KSE imposes a t+1 matching system, even though the matching is completed at the time of trade execution utilising the SMATS on the lock-in basis. As for shares executed manually on the trading floor, member firms confirm the trade details sent to their office through trade confirmation system upon the completion of each transaction by the KSE clerk. Immobilisation has been adopted in Korea, and dematerialisation has been permitted on a limited basis. The Korean commercial code, the basic law on commercial and corporate matters, imposes some limitations on dematerialisation of shares. At issuing market, the securities shall be delivered to investors in the form of securities certificates.

However, once the securities are issued, they can be dematerialised by the request of investor or KSSC acting as a nominee to issuing companies. Approximately, 60 per cent of the shares deposited in the KSSC are dematerialised. Member firms are prohibited from entrusting the settlement of securities transactions to institutions not designated by KSE. Member firms are required to deposit with the KSSC at least 90 per cent of the shares held in their own accounts as well as those of their customers to facilitate the central depository function of the KSSC. Of the six DAEs, the Korean market enjoys the most efficient and well-developed centralised clearing and settlement systems. The *KSE Fact Book* (1990) reported that 1.5 billion shares of the total trading volume of 3.4 billion shares was netted out, leaving 1.9 billion shares to be cleared through the book-entry system. Of the total cleared, 99.2 per cent or 1.89 billion shares were settled by way of book-entry deliveries.

A guarantee fund called the Joint Compensation Fund (JCF) has been set up and administered by the KSE. The fund is used to cover any losses resulting from unsettled transactions. The rate of deposit paid into the fund by each member is 1/100 000 of its trading value, but the amount of contribution is limited to a maximum of 2/300 of the trading value per member in the previous year. Additional protection is provided by Fidelity Guaranty Money, even though it is relatively small. All members are required to deposit fidelity guaranty money in an amount determined by the KSE up to a maximum of W 50 million (US$74 000). The KSE may apply the defaulting member's fidelity guaranty money to fulfill the obligation.

The separation between the KLSE and the SES became effective on 1st January 1990. During a three-month period surrounding the final "split," the trading volume and value at the KLSE recorded about twice the historical averages, even though they declined gradually to the previous level. The SCANS, a wholly owned subsidiary of KLSE, introduced the daily netting system. This system represented a drastic change from the traditional weekly netting which was implemented under the rolling system over a two-week period with a t+8 settlement. The daily netting system did not succeed since clearing members had difficulties in tracking the movement of share certificates. The main reason for this new system's failure may have been the lack of central depository function. As an interim step toward a full-fledged central depository system, a new settlement system called the Fixed Delivery and Settlement System (FDSS) was introduced in February 1990. Under the FDSS, the date for delivery of scrip and settlement is t+5, and scrip sent to SCANS for clearing and settlement is immobilised for safekeeping in SCANS' vaults to reduce its physical movement to and from SCANS unless the broker or his clients request otherwise.

A new company, the Malaysian Central Depository Sdn. Bhd. (MCD), has been set up to implement a full-fledged central depository system in 1991 following recommendations made by the G-30 for domestic clearing and settlement and by the FIBV for cross-border clearing and settlement. The MCD will provide depository services to anyone owning securities listed on the KLSE. These services will be made available to the general public through direct members of MCD which will include: (a) KLSE member companies; (b) banks, merchant banks, or finance houses; (c) KLSE/SCANS; (d) institutional investors; (e) fund managers; (f) registrars; and (g) issuing houses. The shareholders of MCD will include KLSE and a wide range of the Malaysian capital market representatives approved by the Ministry of Finance to ensure the independence of MCD's operation. Following the implementation of a central depository system, physical delivery will no longer be a permissible method of settlement. Thus, investors in the KLSE will find it necessary to use CDS in order to trade after the initial 18-month period.[23]

A book-entry-based settlement and clearing system has been applied to transactions in the SESDAQ securities and securities of newly listed companies. Since June 1991, the SES has commenced converting the existing listed companies from the scrip-based to the book-based settlement system. The SES plans to bring all existing main board issues under the scripless system over the next two years. The SES has adopted the immobilisation approach for its book-entry settlement system. As trades have to be matched by the computer before they are executed, completion of matching is instantaneous on the date of transaction. As far as securities settled on the scrip-based system are concerned, clearing of trades is done by the Securities Clearing and Computer Services (Pte) Ltd. (SCCS), while all securities settled on the book-based system are cleared by the Central Depository Pte Ltd. (CDP), a wholly owned subsidiary of the SES. Under the present system, the SES classifies securities trading into four categories: (a) ready-market transactions comprise the main volume of trading with a settlement time of seven (calendar) days, after which the seller must deliver his scrip to the brokerage firm and the buyer must pick up his or scrip; (b) cash market transactions require same-day settlement; (c) buying-in-market transactions are used to "buy-in" shares for which trades were previously made with no timely settlement made. The same-day settlement rule applies; and (d) odd-lot market trades in odd-sized blocks of stocks follow the same settlement rule as ready-market transactions.

The CDP operates a traditional depository and book-entry transfer system for the securities market in Singapore. It guarantees the settlement of all member companies' trades; i.e., if a member company defaults in delivery or payment, the CDP will honor all the obligations of the defaulting member company to the other member companies. As part of its clearing services, the CDP provides reporting and affirmation of institutional trades through the Institutional Delivery and Affirmation System (IDAS). An individual investor opens either a direct securities account with the CDP or a sub-account with a depository agent who may be a member company of the SES, a trust company, or a bank's nominee registered with CDP. The CDP has a paid-up capital of S\$2 million (US\$1.05 million), and it maintains a clearing fund to make good losses suffered by the CDP as a result of the failure of any clearing member to perform its obligations or to make any required payment to the CDP. The base deposit of each clearing member to the clearing fund is S\$500 000 (US\$0.26 million) and a "variable deposit" is calculated for each clearing member based upon the historical amount of business transacted by the member. Additionally, the CDP has a lien on all long positions and securities in each clearing member's own securities account as security for all of the clearing member's obligations to the CDP.

In Taiwan the settlement date of equity shares and corporate bonds trading is t+2. The transactions of government bonds are settled on the same day, except for those traded on Saturday which are settled on t+1. All trades are compared and matched on a real-time basis using the TSEC's CATS. The Taiwan Securities Central Depository Co., Ltd. (TSCD), which is owned by the TSEC, the Fu-Hua Securities

Finance Corporation, and securities firms, started its operation on 4th January 1990, to handle a centralised securities depository and book-entry clearing and settlement. Its capital is NT$1 billion (US$36.4 million). The operation of TSCD is completely computerised. Each securities firm has at least four terminals on-line with TSCD, with at least 1,550 terminals running the entire system. Currently, both physical settlement and book-entry settlement are handled by TSCD, with physical settlement being phased out. During the first year of operation, TSCD reported that about 90 per cent of trading accounts are settled through book-entry settlement. In terms of trading value, approximately three-quarters are settled by the book-entry system.[24] Complete immobilisation of securities may have to wait a while in light of the fact that only 26 per cent of listed securities certificates are safekeeping at TSCD. The TSCD also provides safekeeping service for certificates and serves as a registrar and transfer agent.

All clearing and settlement at the SET take place in the afternoon of t+3 day after initial transactions by Thai domestic investors. The trade comparison takes place on the trading day t. Under the current clearing procedures, the transactions are "locked" in on t+2 after initial validation, while the selling customer is required to deliver the share certificate to his broker no later than 12 noon on t+1. However, foreign investors are allowed to settle on t+7. The clearing function is provided by the Share Depository Division of SET, while the depository function is conducted by the Share Depository Center (SDC) which was established in January 1988 to eliminate physical delivery of share certificates. The SDC provides services of deposit and withdrawal for 197 securities authorised by SET in the capacity of share registrar. Approximately 90 per cent of transactions are handled by the SDC's book-entry system and the remaining 10 per cent by the physical delivery system. Currently, only those transactions on the special and foreign boards are allowed to be handled by the physical delivery system. The daily netting successfully reduced the number of payments and deliveries between SET member firms: A total of 5,400 deliveries per day was reduced to 800 in 1989 and 2,700 deliveries were reduced to 450 in 1990.

The SDC plans to expand its services not only to member firms but also to other securities firms which are non-members, custodian banks, and other institutional investors such as insurance companies and investment trusts to further reduce the costs associated with share transfer and safekeeping. The SDC also proposes a change in the legal framework to make it possible to deposit and register shares under its SDC's own name. Once the change is effected, every beneficial shareholder will be able to exercise his rights directly in the name of the brokerage firm. Additionally, the securities deposited with SDC could be sold at any time, whereas they cannot be sold when the transfer of title is in progress. Also for the convenience of foreign investors, the SDC works on the establishment of custodial linkages with central depositories of foreign countries. Cross-border clearing and settlement in the Asian region are of immediate interest to SET because more than one-half of foreign investors in the Thai securities market are from Japan, Hong Kong, and Singapore.[25]

Table II. Clearing and settlement systems in six DAEs
(As of December 1989)

	Hong Kong	Korea	Malaysia	Singapore	Taiwan	Thailand
Matching (or comparison) method	One-sided	Two-sided with locked-in feature	Two sided with locked-in feature	Two-sided with locked-in feature	Two-sided with locked-in feature	Two-sided with locked-in feature
Settlement Date	t+1	t+2	t+5	t+5	t+2	t+3
Settlement method	Physical delivery	Book-entry	Both methods	Both methods	Both methods	Both methods
Trade netting method	n.a.	Multilateral netting	Multilateral netting	Multilateral netting	Multilateral netting	Multilateral netting
Centralised clearing body	n.a.	KSSC	SCANS	SCCS	TSCD	SET
Centralised depository	n.a.	KSSC	MCD	CDP	TSCD	SDC
Securities lending and borrowing	n.a.	n.a.	n.a.	n.a.	Yes	n.a.
Guarantee fund	Yes	Yes	n.a.	Yes	Yes	n.a.

Table II summarises the current status of clearing and settlement systems in the six DAES. Substantial progress has been made in all six DAEs for the improvement of clearing and settlement systems with the automation of their securities markets. Korea's centralised system adopted in 1974 has served as a role model of clearing and settlement in the region. The implementation of G-30's nine recommendations and the FIBV's four recommendations by the six DAEs could be completed in the near future even though the suggested timetable may not be strictly followed. Note that clearance, settlement, and depository functions tend to be integrated in a single organisation in the six DAEs. In cases where they are not, the separate organisations are owned by organised exchanges. When all these functions are handled within one organisation, they must be separated for risk-management purposes. Arrangements for the guarantee fund are not clearly defined in Malaysia, while Thailand did not set up the fund. Two countries rely on the surveillance system to maintain the integrity of clearing, settlement, and depository systems. For those countries with guarantee fund arrangements, a careful evaluation of its size is warranted. No regulatory framework is in place for securities lending and borrowing in the six DAEs. Since October 1990, Taiwan securities firms could apply for securities financing business. However, securities lending/borrowing is not yet formally formalised in Taiwan. Although Korea has securities lending system for short selling, no securities borrowing/ lending is allowed to facilitate securities settlement. Currently, Korea and Taiwan evaluate the feasibility of introducing equity derivative products, mainly index futures and index options, in their respective markets. There will be clear advantages to establishing close co-ordination between the corresponding clearing and settlement arrangements in equity and equity derivative markets.

A few important lessons can be learned from the failure Hong Kong's futures market in October 1987. With the launching of the Hang Seng Index futures in May 1986, the Hong Kong Commodity Futures Exchange was renamed the Hong Kong Futures Exchange (HKFE) without improving the institutional structure of the local futures market. As brokerage firms and institutional investors in Hong Kong were quick to incorporate Hang Seng Index futures contracts into their portfolio management, the trading volume skyrocketed, exceeding the other futures contracts written on soybeans, sugar and gold. (In February 1991, a new interest rate futures contract written on the Hong Kong Interbank Offered Rate for three-month deposits was introduced.) Prior to the market 1987 market crash, trading of the Hang Seng Index futures accounted more that 90 per cent of HKFE's total trading value. However, as the SRC Report correctly pointed out, trading activity had far outstripped the capacity and capability of the risk control arrangements at the HKFE, the International Commodities Clearing House (ICCH), and the Hong Kong Futures Guarantee Corporation (FGC). For some dubious historical reasons, the clearing and guarantee functions were contracted out to ICCH and FGC. As a result, there were three independent bodies for the futures market. Their functional responsibilities were loosely defined by: (a) a Deed of Appointment dated 1st December 1985 between ICCH and HKFE; and (b) an Appointment and Management Agreement dated 15th November 1985 between ICCH and FGC. The HKFE set the entry requirements for members, undertook supervision including surveillance of the market, and set minimum margin for brokers to levy on clients. The ICCH operated the clearing and matching functions, while the FGC was supposed to guarantees trades and decided on margin calls.

The SRC Report cited many structural weaknesses in the risk management system:

(a)   no direct legal relationship between HKFE and FGC;

(b)   no direct relationship between FGC and clearing members;

(c)   no risk exposure of ICCH as part of its clearing role;

(d)   inadequate guarantee arrangements;

(e)   inadequate margin enforcement;

(f)   inadequate capital requirement for HKFE members;

(g)   lack of clearing house involvement in active day-to-day monitoring and surveillance; and

(h)   lack of participation of clearing members in management of clearing house.

In the light of the ineffective tripartite structure of the futures market, the SRC recommended that: (a) a clearing house be incorporated as a wholly-owned subsidiary of the HKFE; (b) the new clearing house serve as a counterparty to every trade that is registered to maintain the integrity of guarantee system; (c) the clearing house's risk be covered by a fund made up of deposits from clearing members and some external means such as a guarantee from a banking syndicate or insurance, or both; (d) clearing members participate in the decision making of the clearing house.

HKFE members approved in May 1989 the reconstitution of the futures exchange and a new clearing house, the HKFE Clearing Corporation Ltd. (HKCC) was established with a new risk management structure along the lines recommended by the SRC. Every HKCC member must be a member of HKFE and two categories of membership were created: (a) general clearing members who are allowed to register and clear trades both on their own accounts and on behalf of non-clearing members and clearing members; and (b) clearing members who are only allowed to register and clear trades on their own behalf. Unlike FGC, HKCC becomes a counterparty to every trade registered with and cleared through it. HKCC has established a reserve fund to meet its obligations as counterparty in circumstances where an HKCC member defaults in its obligations to HKCC. The fund is made up from money and/or facilities such as: (a) members' deposits; (b) other resources appropriated by HKCC to the fund out of the general revenue of HKCC; (c) insurance arranged for the purpose of supporting the fund; and (d) bank guarantees or other facilities arranged for the purpose of supporting the fund. HKCC was given a number of powers which it can use to assist in the risk management process. They include: (a) the power to demand margin and to increase margin when necessary; (b) daily adjustment of contracts by equity margining or "marking-to-market"; (c) the power to require additional margin; and (d) the power to impose position limits. The new risk management structure was tested as the Hang Seng Index futures contracts fluctuated significantly in response to events in May and June 1989. The index fell 339 points on 22nd May, gained 261 on 23rd May, fell 256 on 25th May, fell 581 on 5th June, and gained 171 on 12th June. HKFE and HKCC raised minimum clearing house margin and customer margin requirements and issued several intra-day margin calls. There was no default by futures brokers to HKCC despite large fluctuations in the price of underlying index. The recent Hong Kong experience in coping with potential systemic risks demonstrates that the efficiency of the risk management system is far more important than the magnitude of guarantee funds.

With the establishment of financial futures markets in Singapore in 1984, the Gold Exchange of Singapore was restructured and renamed SIMEX. The SIMEX currently offers ten types of futures contracts written on: (a) Nikkei Stock Average; (b) Three-month Eurodollar; (c) Three-month Euroyen; (d) Three-month Euromark; (e) Dubai Crude Oil; (f) High Sulphur Fuel Oil; (g) Japanese Yen; (h) Deutschemark; (i) British Pound; and (j) Gold. It also offers four types of options written on: (a) Eurodollar Futures; (b) Euroyen Futures; (c) Japanese Yen Futures; and (d) Deutschemark. SIMEX and the Chicago Mercantile Exchange (CME) established a linked clearing programme, the Mutual Offset System (MOS). Through this system, positions opened on one exchange can be offset ("closed") on the other exchange. Thus, SIMEX members can execute trades on the CME and then transfer those trades back to SIMEX as new or liquidating trades. Likewise, CME members can execute trades on SIMEX and then have those trades transferred back to the CME. Currently, the MOS is in effect for Eurodollar, Deutschemark, Japanese Yen and British Pound futures contracts. SIMEX has four membership categories: three categories of corporate members and one category of individual members. They are: (a) corporate clearing member; (b) corporate non-clearing member; (c) commercial associate member; and (d) individual non-clearing member. Corporate clearing members own one share and three seats on the SIMEX. They are entitled to full trading rights on the trading floor, accept customers' business, and clear trades. Corporate non-clearing members own three seats on SIMEX. They are also entitled to trading rights on the trading floor, accept customers' business, but does not have authority to clear trades. Commercial associate members' trading rights are limited to energy futures contracts only. They may trade only for their own accounts and those of related and associated companies, but are not allowed to clear trades. Individual non-clearing members have full trading rights on the trading floor, but trade only for their own accounts. They own or lease one seat or obtain a trading permit which allows trading on energy contracts only. SIMEX specify the minimum financial requirements for each membership category. For example, a corporate clearing member must maintain a minimum paid-up capital of S$2 million (US$1.05 million), and adjusted net capital of not less than S$4 million (US$2.10 million) or 10 per cent of customer funds. In addition to the minimum financial requirements, the clearing member must maintain a special reserve fund to which part of net profits must be transferred so long as the total amount of paid up capital and the special reserve fund is less than S$5 million (US$2.63 million). A corporate non-clearing member must maintain a S$1 million (US$0.53 million) minimum paid-up capital and net tangible assets of S$1 million (US$0.53 million). The net adjusted capital for a commercial associate member is S$25 000 (US$13 200). However, a commercial associate member must deposit with the exchange an irrevocable letter of credit of not less than S$1 million (US$0.53 million). SIMEX imposes the cross margin system which requires all clearing members to maintain margins with the clearing house for house positions separately from customers' positions. In addition, margins for customers' positions are computed on gross basis without allowing, for example, one customer's long positions to offset another's short positions.

The SIMEX has adopted the CME model in its operational model which has an in-house clearing function as part of its risk management systems. Therefore, the clearing house is part of SIMEX under the control of the House Clearing Committee. In contrast, the Chicago Board of Trade (CBOT) clearing house is outside the exchange. In the light of the experiences at CME and CBOT, either structure would work as long as the risk management systems are well co-ordinated under self-regulatory processes. During the 1987 market crash, SIMEX was also severely tested by the spill-over of the stock market volatility into the futures market. SIMEX's risk management systems stood the test and all margin requirements including intra-day margin calls were met by clearing members without any serious incidents.

Chapter VI

Securities market regulation

A. Regulatory coverage

The Brady Commission proposed that one agency must have the authority to regulate all financial markets in the belief that: (a) markets for equity and equity derivative products are in fact one market; and (b) the market break in October 1987 can be traced to failure of these market segments to act as one. This recommendation was supported by the Smith Panel. A similar recommendation was made by the SRC to improve the operation and regulation of the Hong Kong securities market. In the wake of a drastic price drop in October 1987, the US regulatory and institutional structures designed independently for various markets were not effective in responding to "inter-market" pressures. The US SEC is responsible for equity and options markets; the CFTC oversees futures market; the Federal Reserve Board has authority over margin regulations; and the stock, futures, and options exchanges have their own rules and regulations for clearing and settlement systems and for monitoring the financial resources of market makers. A similar problem caused by the lack of co-ordination among regulatory bodies was observed in the Hong Kong securities markets. Regulatory powers were divided between the Securities Commission, the Commodities Trading Commission, and their executive arm, the Commissioner for Securities and Commodities Trading, in an ad hoc manner without any integrated structure, centralised management, or financial resources prior to the 1987 market break in Hong Kong. As a result, the SRC proposed replacement of the two commissions and the commissioner's office with a single independent statutory body outside the civil service.

At present, it is not clear whether the "one market, one agency" recommendation will be implemented in the United States. However, on the basis of the SRC recommendation, a new supervisory body called the SFC has been formed in Hong Kong. The SFC was formally established in May 1989. As a statutory regulator, the SFC serves as a "watchdog" to promote orderly securities and futures markets in Hong Kong. The future success of the new regulatory structure is dependent upon an effective and co-operative working relationship among the SFC, the SEHK, its 22-member Exchange Council, and the HKFE. It is premature to judge the success of the new structure because it has been in operation no more than two years in Hong

Kong. Although the Hong Kong market is in need of sound regulatory structures, some have suggested that many regulatory measures for further improvement of the financial system of Hong Kong, mostly initiated by the SFC, may be "regulatory overkill."

A number of scholars and practitioners expressed dissatisfaction with the "one market, one agency" recommendation. For example, Fischel (1989) stressed that the entire Brady Commission report failed to show a single shred of evidence that regulatory failure produced or exacerbated the October market crash. The one-agency proposal, he further suggested, implies that competition among regulatory agencies is harmful; the consensus supports the opposite. Miller (1990) criticised that "one agency" regulation was proposed on the basis of little more than the majority's gut feelings rather than on a thorough sifting of the evidence. Melamed (1990) echoed Miller's criticism. Both Miller and Melamed served on the Smith Panel.[26]

The overall regulatory structures in Korea, Singapore, and Taiwan are consistent with the "one agency" format. The MOFs and the SECs in Korea and Taiwan have complete authority over formulation and implementation of securities market policies. When futures and options contracts are introduced, it is unlikely that the two countries would adopt regulatory structures similar to those in the United States. Rather it is expected that some variations of the Japanese model in which the equity market and the equity derivative market are integrated are likely to be followed. Substantial changes in the government regulation of the securities market of Singapore were undertaken not after the 1987 market crash but after the Pan-Electric Industries crisis in 1985. Six member companies became insolvent due to collapsed stock prices and exposure to forward contracts after the failure of the Pan-Electric Industries. The Securities Industry Act was revised in 1986 to strengthen supervisory and regulatory functions of the MAS over the SES's operation and the securities industry. The rules of the SES were amended to place heavier emphasis on capital requirements, financial structure, and monitoring processes of securities firms. The MAS performs all the traditional functions of a central bank except for the issue of currency. It is also given power to regulate and control the stock and futures markets. An extreme form of regulatory fragmentation is observed in Malaysia. There are four regulatory bodies representing three Ministries of the Malaysian government. The CIC, under the MOF, oversees the issue of securities and the approval of company share listings on the KLSE. The Registrar of Companies (ROC) under the Ministry of Trade and Industry administers and regulates the securities Industry Act. Listed companies conducting a public offering must register a prospectus and other disclosure documents. The ROC is also empowered to issue, renew, or reject licenses to dealers, dealer's representatives, and investment advisors. It implements measures to protect the market from unfair practices. The Foreign Investment Committee (FIC) under the Prime Minister's Department implements the guidelines on regulation of assets or interests, mergers or takeovers of companies and businesses, and is responsible for major issues on foreign investment. The Panel on Take-overs and Mergers (TOP) oversees all takeovers and mergers to ensure that they are conducted in an orderly manner. Additionally, the issue of corporate bonds requires an approval from the Bank Negara Malaysia, which also has sole responsibility for government securities markets. Fragmentation of authority as evidenced in Malaysia can prove very costly for its capital market development. To a lesser extent, Thailand shows a similar weakness. Currently the SET is regulated by the MOF and the BOT. The MOF does not have a special supervisory agency to regulate the SET. In practice, supervision of financial institutions is delegated to BOT. BOT's supervisory function is carried out by the Departments of Financial Institution Supervision and Examination. Both Malaysia and Thailand should review the feasibility of creating an agency similar to the SEC with full regulatory authority over registration, supervision, licensing, and examination functions, while leaving operational responsibility of the securities markets to KLSE and SET.

Another important regulatory issue was introduced by the diminishing distinctions between commercial banks and securities companies. In universal banking countries such as Germany and Switzerland, securities and investment banking businesses are treated as traditional banking activities. In contrast, the Glass-Steagall Act of the United States and Article 65 of the Securities and Exchange Law of Japan separate banking business from securities business. In recent years, however, this barrier has been falling down. German and Swiss banks have established securities business subsidiaries in the United States and Japan. In return, US and Japanese brokerage houses have started banking subsidiaries in Germany and Switzerland. London banking subsidiaries of US securities companies have opened branch offices in Japan to conduct banking business, while Japanese banks have purchased equity ownership of US investment banking houses. All these cross-border activities and divergent regulatory arrangements create serious gaps in regulatory coverage. One distinct possibility is that substantial risk exposure by subsidiaries or affiliates of any banking or securities company may be left unsupervised. On a limited scale, similar developments occurred in some of the six DAEs. In Korea, for example, the Korea Development Bank, one of premier development finance institutes, was recently authorised to engage in the securities business. Four large commercial banks were allowed to become SES members as part of the government's efforts to strengthen the securities industry after the 1985 market crisis in Singapore.

B. Internationalisation of securities markets and regulatory implications

The governments of the six DAEs have been implementing plans for internationalisation of their securities markets and securities industry. For example, in October 1990, the SES created a new category of membership called "international membership" to allow foreign securities firms to engage in brokerage business for both resident and non-resident investors. Transactions for resident investors are restricted to not less than S$5 million (US$2.63 million). The SES signed a custodial agreement with the Japan Securities Clearing Corporation (JSCC) to facilitate book-entry settlement for trading in Japanese securities. Under the agreement, share certificates owned by investors in the CDP account will be immobilised and kept in a CDP account with JSCC. JSCC will administer the shareholder entitlements such as dividends for investors. Foreign investors have access to the Korean market indirectly through: (a) 13 international investment trusts with a combined capital of US$595 million; (b) three "matching unit trusts" with a combined capital of US$300 million which are invested in both Korean and foreign securities; (c) three international closed-end investment companies with a total capital of US$360 million; (d) 10 convertible bonds in the amount of US$320 million; and (e) two corporate bonds with warrants in the amount of 120 million. The government relaxed foreign exchange controls to allow Korean institutional investors to hold foreign currency denominated securities. Each company is allowed to invest up to US$30 million. As part of internationalising the Korean securities industry, foreign securities companies are allowed to set up branch offices in Seoul and to form joint ventures with Korean partners. Foreign investment in Thailand amounted to B 97.28 billion (US$3.87 billion) or 12.90 per cent of total market capitalisation in 1989. The SET is studying the feasibility of establishing a custodial linkage with foreign central depository bodies in the Asian region for a scripless cross-border trading. Beginning in January 1991, foreign institutional investors have been allowed to invest in the TSEC-listed securities. Each individual foreign institution is permitted to invest in the range of US$5 million to US$50 million. All foreign investors, however, must observe the maximum limit not exceeding 10 per cent of a listed firm's capital, and each single institution shall not exceed 5 per cent. Additionally, the Securities and Exchange Law will be revised to allow local securities companies to act as agents to buy and sell foreign securities, to establish branch offices abroad, or to register as members of foreign stock exchanges. To expand the outbound investment channels for residents, four securities investment trust companies are allowed to raise local capital (US$40 million each) for the purpose of investing in foreign securities. Since 1990, residents of Taiwan have been allowed to remit in and abroad up to US$ 3 million per capita or its equivalent in other currencies. To facilitate foreign exchange risk hedging, a forward foreign exchange market was opened on 1st November 1991.

As the globalisation of the DAEs' securities markets progresses, potential risks of contagion are also increasing. The failure of individual securities companies in one country may lead to chain reactions that could be detrimental to the achievement of systemic stability in the region. Hence, supervision and regulation on a national level would not be sufficient unless international co-ordination is undertaken. Harmonization of national supervisory activities emerges as an important task. The establishment of a framework for co-ordinating supervisory activities and for exchanging necessary information is needed more than ever. Kane (1991) correctly emphasized that globalisation is better seen as a process in which increasing international competition imposes *market discipline* on government regulators even though this discipline constricts the freedom of financial regulators in different countries.

Chapter VII

Capital Adequacy of Securities Firms

The market crash in October 1987 stimulated a renewed interest in the capital adequacy of securities firms. The most important report relevant to this issue was produced by the Technical Committee of the International Organisation of Securities Commissions (IOSCO). The report is entitled "Capital Adequacy Standards for Securities Firms" and was officially adopted by IOSCO at its 14th Annual Conference in Venice, Italy, on 18th-21st September 1989. The report represents a critically important effort to harmonize capital requirements for securities firms in conjunction with the 1988 report by the Basle Committee on Banking Regulations and Supervisory Practices on "International Convergence of Capital Measurement and Capital Standards" for banking firms. The issue of capital adequacy of securities firms in the six DAEs is evaluated against the backdrop of recommendations by the IOSCO report.

The IOSCO report made the following recommendations for capital adequacy standards.

a) A common conceptual framework regarding the capital requirements for securities firms is needed.

b) The framework should contain the following elements: (i) the coverage of liquidity and solvency needs; (ii) marking-to-market of marketable securities and commodities positions; and (iii) the enforcement of risk-based capital requirements.

c) The definition of capital should reflect the fluctuating nature of risk-based requirements and the differing regulatory structures of member countries.

d) Differing minimum capital requirements should be established based on a firm's type of business, but capital requirements should not be set so high as to adversely affect competition in the marketplace.

e) Capital requirements should be reinforced by adequate record keeping, reporting, and examination programmes.

The IOSCO report further outlines a three-part conceptual framework against which capital adequacy standards for securities firms can be measured. The framework includes: (a) a capital adequacy test that reflects liquidity, solvency, and market and settlement risks faced by a securities firm[27]; (b) a regulatory structure for the maintenance of a securities firm's books and records; and (c) a reporting system to and examination by a supervisory authority. The first part of the framework addresses the issue of capital adequacy, whereas the last two parts deal more with the regulatory aspect of actual implementation. Unlike banking firms that take long-term investment positions, securities firms take short-term positions. Thus, securities firms are more vulnerable to short-term fluctuations of securities price movement, while credit risk is the predominant risk faced by banking firms.

In connection with approaches to capital adequacy, the IOSCO recognises two different approaches to addressing liquidity and solvency, but it did not recommend any particular approach over another. The first approach uses a combined test of liquidity and solvency, under which a securities firm is required to maintain net liquid assets which exceed its total liabilities by a sufficient margin to cover the net worth of the firm. Net liquid assets should not include intangible, non-marketable, and illiquid assets, or most unsecured receivables. An alternative approach introduces two separate requirements, one for liquidity and another for solvency. Under this approach, a securities firm must maintain a certain ratio of liquid assets to short-term liabilities purely for working capital management and a separate solvency test ratio to protect its net worth. However, both approaches recommend marking-to-market for securities and commodities held by securities firms. Additionally, the IOSCO strongly favours the adoption of risk-based requirements to cover market and settlement risks with a sufficient cushion of capital to cover immeasurable risks. The risk-based requirements have a definite advantage over traditional flat minimum capital requirements across the border.

There were two categories of membership at the SEHK: individual and corporate. At the end of June 1990, the SEHK had 702 members. Of the 702 members, 141 were corporate members and 561 were individual members. Right after the October 1987 market crash, there were 738 members with 83 corporate members and 655 individual members. The SRC identified three weaknesses of the SEHK membership. First, the number of SEHK members was too large relative to the size of the market, resulting in fierce competition and undesirable trade practices. Second, the rules regarding admission of members were inadequate. Third, the net capital and liquidity requirements were inappropriate since they were inflexible and did not reflect risk exposure of individual members (resulting from an unregulated, widespread margin trading). In relation to the third weakness, the SRC recommended that:

a)   the SFC be authorised to set basic minimum net capital (= the excess of approved assets over ranking liabilities) and liquidity margin (= the excess of liquid assets over ranking liabilities) for securities (and futures) intermediaries; and

b)   the capital requirements be determined by the nature of brokers' business, their volume of business, and their risk exposure.

The SFC has been reviewing present financial resources rules to determine their suitability for Hong Kong, with a view to recommending a new framework to govern capital adequacy for registered HKSE members. The results of this review are expected to be available to the public in the near future. The current net capital requirement is HK$5 million (US$0.64 million) for a corporate member and

HK$1 million (US$0.13 million) for others.[28] Each member is required to maintain a liquidity margin of not less than 10 per cent of the minimum net capital requirements described above.

Under the Korean Securities and Exchange Law, the securities business is classified into three categories: dealing, brokerage, and underwriting. In addition to the three categories of activities, Korean securities firms, with approval from the MOF, may engage in other activities such as the extension of credit for securities transactions, securities savings business, payment guarantee for corporate bonds, trading of bonds with repurchase agreement and negotiable certificates of deposit, and an overseas securities business. Securities dealing transactions are conducted at the securities firms' own risk in bonds, unlisted stocks, or odd-lots in the OTC market. In the brokerage business, a securities firm trades securities in its own name for its customers and virtually all listed stocks are traded on a brokerage basis. According to the Korean underwriting practice, the underwriter purchases all stocks or government-issued bonds in total. Only for corporate bonds, the underwriter solicits subscription and absorbs the unsold portion to complete the subscription.

The minimum capital requirement varies depending upon the number of securities business categories in which a firm intends to engage: (a) W 500 million (US$0.74 million) for one category; (b) W 2 billion (US$2.96 million) for two categories; and (c) W 3 billion (US$4.44 million) for all three categories. Korea has 25 licensed securities firms, and they are all members of the KSE. At the present time, 24 of the 25 KSE member firms are licensed to conduct all three categories of business. The average capital stock per member firm in 1989 amounted to US$148 million. Financial intermediaries, including banks, investment trust companies, short-term finance companies, and merchant banking corporations may engage in underwriting business, but they are not qualified as KSE members. Additionally, with approval from the MOF, a securities firm with capital of W 20 billion (US$29.63 million) or more may conduct securities business overseas, business of payment guarantees for corporate bonds, and business of trading negotiable certificates of deposit. The minimum capital requirement for a securities firm eligible to become a manager in underwriting stocks and corporate bonds (excluding guaranteed and mortgage bonds) is W 7 billion (US$10.37 million) in both paid-in and equity capital; and W 5 billion (US$7.41 million) for all other bonds. No individuals, partnerships, or legal entities other than stock companies may be licensed as a securities firm. To ensure the soundness of the financial structure of securities firms, the SEC and KSE monitor financial performance. The amount of net working capital of a securities firm may not be less than W 150 million (US$0.22 million) to conduct one category of the securities business, W 500 million (US$0.74 million) for two categories, and W 600 million (US$0.89 million) for all three categories. The average size of net working capital of KSE member firms was US$355 million as of December 1989. A securities firm is required to maintain a debt-to-net asset ratio of no more than 10. It is also required to set aside reserves in proportion to the trading volume of securities and sales profit to make up for any losses incurred from securities transactions.

The securities business in Malaysia is carried out by member companies either with limited or unlimited liability. Members of the KLSE are either individuals or corporations who shall be the shareholders of the member companies. The member companies are generally small. Depending upon the locality, all member companies are required to have a paid-up capital of at least M$20 million (US$7.41 million) by the end of 1991. Thus, with the encouragement of the Ministry of Finance and the KLSE, member companies initiated various restructuring options, such as merging with other member companies, going public on the KLSE's main board, and inviting equity participation of eligible corporations either local or foreign. As of June 1990, the KLSE has 53 member companies, of which only 46 are active, and 148 members, which include 12 corporate members.[29]

Member firms and member companies shall maintain liquid funds: (a) no less than M$100 000 (US$37 000) for each partner of a member firm or director or corporate nominee, and M$50 000 (US$18 500) for each dealer's representative; or (b) an amount that is equivalent to four times the monthly net brokerage earned (= gross brokerage less rebates permitted), whichever is greater.

The SES has a total of 29 corporate members, of which 26 are active. A member company may be an unlimited or limited liability company. The minimum paid-in capital shall not be less than S$10 million (US$5.26 million) or such other amount as determined by the SES. Each member company shall submit to the SES by the 14th day of each month statements of assets and liabilities, adjusted net capital (ANC), and aggregated indebtedness.[30] Recently, the ANC and the aggregate indebtedness/ANC ratio have been amended to S$3 million (US$1.58 million) and 500 per cent, respectively. The 1986 Securities Industry Act and Regulations introduced many new measures to reinforce the financial soundness of securities firms. The dealer's license of a member company will lapse if: (a) its aggregate indebtedness exceeds 1,200 per cent of its ANC; or (b) its ANC falls below S$250 000 (US$132 000) for four consecutive weeks. If the firm's aggregate indebtedness is more than 500 per cent of its ANC, or if its ANC is less than S$3 million (US$1.58 million), the firm should notify the SES which will tell the firm how to operate its business if this state of affairs continues for five consecutive days. Other measures introduced for the protection of SES members include: (a) exposure to a single brokerage client cannot exceed 30 per cent of the firm's average ANC; (b) exposure to a single security cannot exceed 300 per cent of the firm's average ANC if the security is quoted on the main section of the SES, 100 per cent of the firm's ANC if the security is quoted otherwise, or 10 per cent if the security is unquoted; and (c) a firm cannot allow the book value of all securities carried on its own accounts, including unmatched open contract and net underwriting, to exceed 150 per cent of its average ANC.

Under the Securities and Exchange Law, the securities business in Taiwan is classified into three categories of activity: (a) underwriting; (b) brokerage; and (c) dealing. A separate license is required for each category. Brokers execute orders only for their customers, but not for their own accounts, whereas dealers execute orders only for their own accounts. Brokerage and dealing activities are separate, but brokers and dealers may engage in underwriting activities. With the recent revision of the Securities and Exchange Law which came into effect in January 1988, the so-called "super" securities companies are presently allowed to engage in all three activities described above. At the end of 1989, there were a total of 247 licensed brokers, of which 231 were private brokerage firms and the remaining 16 were the trust and savings departments of commercial banks. Of the 231 private brokerage firms, 23 belong to the "super" securities firms. A total of 32 dealers were in business, but their combined transaction volume accounted for only 0.39 per cent of the total 1989 volume. Compare this figure with 95.14 per cent by private brokers and 4.47 per cent by bank brokers. The total number of customer accounts with private and bank brokers increased from 439 904 in 1985 to 4 208 534 in 1989, with an annual compound growth rate of over 75 per cent!

The minimum capital requirements for securities firms are set according to the type of business: (a) NT$400 million (US$15.28 million) for underwriters; (b) NT$200 million (US$7.64 million) for brokers; and (c) NT$400 million (US$15.28 million) for dealers.

Membership in the SET is limited to securities companies licensed by the Ministry of Finance to engage in the securities business. At the end of 1989, the SET had 35 member companies. Securities companies engaged in brokerage, dealing, and investment advisory activities are required to have a registered capital of not less than B 5 million (US$0.20 million), whereas those engaged in underwriting must have a registered capital of not less than B 10 million (US$0.40 million). The BOT recognises the inadequacy of the minimum capital requirement for the Thai securities companies. Based on the risk exposure of the securities companies engaged in a full range of securities businesses, a substantial increase in the capital requirement is under study.

Table III presents summary statistics of the capital adequacy of exchange member firms in the six DAEs. The issue of capital adequacy in the six DAEs may not be as serious in countries which adopted the market maker system. Nevertheless, it would be prudent to take protective measures for the main players in the securities markets. The most urgent agenda for the six DAEs is the establishment of a risk-based capital plan for securities firms. This aspect of risk management is seriously lacking in the DAEs, with the exception of Singapore. In Singapore, ANC takes into account the risk profile of securities companies, since securities are marked-to-market daily and losses, including provisions, are deducted from capital so as to obtain ANC positions of the securities companies. In contrast, the minimum capital requirements in Thailand must be revised upward, while those in Taiwan appear relatively high. Unfortunately, it is difficult to declare how high is "high" and how low is "low". This is an important issue which should be examined not only on the national level but also on the international level. Another unresolved issue concerns the capital adequacy of non-corporate members who play active roles in the brokerage business as observed in Hong Kong and Malaysia. Table III summarises minimum capital requirements for corporate members only. Although this is not an issue for all DAEs, an international effort will be needed to examine potential implications. This is particularly so as the region's securities markets as well as its industries lift legal and institutional barriers.

Table III. Summary statistics of member firms (As of December 1989)

	Hong Kong	Korea	Malaysia	Singapore	Taiwan	Thailand
Number of member firms	141	25	53	29	247	35
Net capital requirements (US$ million)	0.64	a. 0.74 b. 2.96 c. 4.44	7.41	5.26	a. 15.28 b. 7.64 c. 15.28	a. 0.20 b. 0.40
Net working capital (US$ million)	0.06	a. 0.22 b. 0.74 c. 0.89	-	0.13	n.a.	-

Notes:

1. The SEHK has 561 individual members in addition to the reported corporate members. The KLSE has 148 individual members in addition to 53 corporate members. Net capital requirements are based on corporate members.

2. Three categories of business are allowed for Korean securities firms: dealing; brokerage; and underwriting. Net capital requirements and net working capital requirements are dependent upon the number of categories in which a firm is engaged. For one category of business, the top figure is the required amount; the middle figure is for two categories of business; and the bottom figure for three categories of business.

3. In Taiwan, net capital requirements vary depending upon the type of securities business in which a firm is engaged. The high amounts are for underwriting business and for dealing; the lower amount is for brokerage business. Regarding net working capital requirements the Securities and Exchange Commission has imposed a restriction that a securities firm's current liabilities can not exceed its current assets.

4. In Thailand, net capital requirements vary depending upon the type of securities business. The tope figure is for brokerage and dealing business and the bottom figure is for underwriters.

5. Net working capital requirements for the KLSE members are dependent upon the number of directors.

6. In October 1990, the SES member's minimum ANC was increased to S$3 million (US$1.58 million).

Notes

1. In addition to the five factors cited, Corrigan included two common denominators: macroeconomic factors and old-fashioned "greed."

2. See Goodhart (1988).

3. Hamao, Masulis, and Ng (1990) reported that the Japanese market is most sensitive to volatility spill-over effects from foreign markets, whereas the US and U.K. markets are only moderately sensitive to volatility spill-overs from foreign stock markets.

4. Goodhart (1988) expressed his doubt about the increasing interdependence of national markets. However, he agreed that the stock market crash of 1987 would be one of the rare instances in which international transmission of volatility was pronounced.

5. The S&P 500 composite index is a value-weighted portfolio of 500 of the largest US firms including 400 industrial, 40 utilities, 40 financials, and 20 transportation companies. The S&P 500 futures contract is one of several financial futures contracts, but it is the most popular futures contract traded on the Chicago Mercantile Exchange (CME).

6. However, the US CFTC's "Final Report on Stock Index Futures and Cash Market Activity During October 1987" (January 1988) cast doubt on the so-called "cascade" theory and the supposition that futures prices were leading the stock market as a reasonable representation of what occurred during the morning of 19th October. The main reason for this doubt was that a significant portion of futures discounts were illusory since a substantial number of stocks in the S&P 500 index were not actively traded.

7. On 19th October there were 187 opening delays, seven trading halts, and three stocks that did not resume trading after halts. On 20th October there were 92 opening delays, 175 trading halts, and ten stocks that did not resume trading. The average opening delay on 19th and 20th October was 1 hour and 35 minutes and 1 hour and 25 minutes, respectively. The average duration of trading halts on 19th and 20th October was 1 hour and 19 minutes and 1 hour and 43 minutes, respectively.

8. The SEHK recently distributed a consultative document entitled "Trading on the Stock Exchange" (October 1990) to solicit opinions from its members and other interested parties.

9. The advertisement of interest is similar to orders except they are not commitments to buy or sell. An advertisement is an indication that a broker (or his customer) is interested in purchasing or selling a particular security if the volume and price of the deal can be negotiated to his satisfaction. Advertisements may only be used on the big lot board, the foreign board, and the cash board.

10. See *SET Automated Project Functional Specification* Volume I (February 1991).

11. Bröker (1991) discusses details of the regulatory implications of market automation.

12. The reported percentages are not included in the KSE's official publications. They are computed by the author for the purpose of comparison with other countries.

13. KSE's daily price limits are similar to those of TSE. The TSE also sets the limits in terms of the yen price level and the unofficial percentage limits range from 6.67 per cent to 50 per cent. This range is wider than those applicable to the KSE-listed stocks.

14. See NYSE's "The Rule 80A Index Arbitrage Tick Test: Interim Report to the US Securities & Exchange Commission" (January 1991).

15. For details, see Morris (1990).

16. See *Overview of Computer-Assisted Trading System at Taiwan Stock Exchange* by Taiwan Stock Exchange Data Processing Center (1990).

17. Margin loans discussed here are assumed to be between broker-dealers and public customers. For example, there are no explicit maintenance margin requirements for margin loans between banks or other lenders and public customers, and between banks and brokers-dealers. Rather, the maintenance margins are handled "on a good-faith basis" which implies that banks or other lenders exercise sound banking judgement. For greater details, see Sofiano (1988).

18. In contrast, margins are very common in futures markets. Any investor with an open position in futures must deposit margin with his broker. Even before an elaborate structure of margin rules was developed by futures exchanges, the forces of competition and brokers' self-interest impelled brokers to set appropriate margins.

19. See Cohen (1966), Largay (1973), and Luckett (1982), among others.

20. See Hardouvelis (1988, 1990) and Hardouvelis and Peristiani (1989).

21. A three-page abstract of Ahn's dissertation written in Korean was made available to the author of this report.

22. The Options Clearing Corporation (OCC) handles clearing and settlement of options, and futures exchanges maintain their own clearing houses.

23. See "Information Paper on Proposed Central Depository System (CDS)" by KLSE and "Central Depository System (CDS): An Introduction for the Market Professional" by MCD.

24. Refer to a speech entitled "Taiwan Stock Exchange in 1990" delivered by S. T. Hsu of TSE at the Fourth Annual Asia Capital Market Conference held in Bangkok in January 1991.

25. Refer to a speech entitled "Settlement Procedure of the Stock Exchange of Thailand," delivered by Phadoongsidhi of the SET on 6th February 1991. The title of the conference at which this speech was delivered is unspecified in the draft.

26. See Appendix H of the "NYSE Market Volatility and Investor Confidence Panel Report."

27. Note that the IOSCO report uses "position risk" to denote "market risk".

28. If an individual member holds more than one share of the SEHK, the net capital requirement increases proportionally. If a corporate member holds not more than five shares, the net capital requirement is HK$5 million (US$0.64 million); otherwise, the net capital requirement equals the number of shares held times HK$1 million (US$0.13 million).

29. According to the KLSE *Rules Relating to Member Firms and Member Companies*, KLSE members may be recognised as either "member firms" that are partnerships which must comply with all the requirements of Rule 3 or "member companies" that are private or public companies with limited liability and subject to Rule 4.

30. Adjusted net capital means shareholders' funds less non-current assets and prepaid expenses; less all unsecured loans and advances that are included as current assets; less all unsecured amounts due from each director; less deficits in clients' accounts and provisions for bad and doubtful debts; less any shortfall in the security values carried in the books.

References

Amihud, Y. and H. Mendelson, "Trading Mechanisms and Stock Returns: An Empirical Investigation," *Journal of Finance* (July 1987), 533-53.

Ahn, K. H., "The Effectiveness of Margin Regulation in the Korean Securities Market: Margin Requirements and Good-Faith Deposit," Unpublished Ph.D. Dissertation (in Korean) at Kunkook University (January 1991).

Becketti, S. and D. J. Roberts, "Will Increased Regulation of Stock Index Futures Reduce Stock Market Volatility?" *Federal Reserve Bank of Kansas City Economic Review* (November/December 1990), 33-46.

Bröker, G., "Automation of Securities Markets and Regulatory Implications", *Financial Market Trends* No. 50, OECD Publications (October 1991).

Chung, J. R., "Price Limit System and Volatility of Korean Stock Markets," *Pacific-Basin Capital Markets Research* Volume II (Edited by S. G. Rhee and R. P. Chang) (Amsterdam: North-Holland, 1991), 283-94.

Cohen, J., "Federal Reserve Margin Requirements and the Stock Market," *Journal of Financial and Quantitative Analysis* (September 1966), 30-54.

Corrigan, E. G., "A Perspective on Recent Financial Disruptions," *FRBNY Quarterly Review* (Winter 1989-90), 8-15.

Domowitz, I., "The Mechanics of Automated Trade Execution Systems," *Journal of Financial Intermediation* (1990), 167-94.

Duffee, G., P. Kupiec, and A. P. White, "A Primer on Program Trading and Stock Price Volatility: A Survey of the Issues and the Evidence," Board of Governors of the Federal Reserve System Working Paper (September 1990).

Edwards, F. R., "Does Futures Trading Increase Stock Volatility?" *Financial Analysts Journal* (January/February 1988a), 63-69.

Edwards, F. R., "Futures Trading and Cash Market Volatility: Stock Index and Interest Rate Futures," *Journal of Futures Markets* 8 (1988b), 421-39.

Edwards, F. R., "Policies to Curb Stock Market Volatility," in *Financial Market Volatility* (Kansas City: Federal Reserve Bank of Kansas City, 1988c), 141-66.

Fama, E. F., "Perspectives on October 1987, or, What Did We Learn from the Crash?" in *Black Monday and the Future of Financial Markets* (Edited by R. W. Kamphuis Jr., R. C. Kormendi, and J. W. Henry Watson) (Homewood, Illinois: Irwin, 1989), 71-82.

Federal Reserve Bank of New York, *The Chicago Mercantile Exchange*, July 1989.

Federal Reserve Bank of New York, *Clearing and Settlement Through Board of Trade Clearing Corporation*, February 1990.

Federal Reserve Bank of New York, *Exchanges and Clearing Houses for Financial Futures and Options in the United Kingdom*, March 1989.

Federal Reserve Bank of New York, *An Overview of the Operations of the Options Clearing Corporation*, April 1989.

Fédération Internationale des Bourses de Valeurs, "Improving International Settlement", A Report of the Task Force Appointed by FIBV (1989).

Ferris, S. and D. Chance, "Margin Requirements and Stock Market Volatility," *Economic Letters* (1988), 251-54.

Fischel, D. R., "Should One Agency Regulate Financial Markets?" in *Black Monday and the Future of Financial Markets* (edited by R. W. Kamphuis Jr., R. C. Kormendi, and J. W. Henry Watson) (Homewood, Illinois: Irwin, 1989), 113-20.

Freris, A. F., "The Effects of the Introduction of Stock Index Futures on Stock Prices: The Experience of Hong Kong 1984-1987," in *Pacific-Basin Capital Markets Research* Volume I (Edited by S. G. Rhee and R. P. Chang) (Amsterdam: North-Holland, 1991), 409-16.

Froot, K. A., J. F. Gammill, Jr., and A. F. Perold, "New Trading Practices and the Short-Run Predictability of the S&P 500," in *Market Volatility and Investor Confidence* (New York, New York Stock Exchange, 1990), G1 1-27.

Furbush, D. "Program Trading and Price Movements Around the October 1987 Market Break," US S.E.C. Working Paper (May 1989).

Gerety, M. S. and J. H. Mulherin, "Patterns in Intraday Stock Market Volatility: Past and Present," US S.E.C. Working Paper (November 1990).

Goodhart, C., "The International Transmission of Asset Price Volatility," in *Financial Market Volatility* (The Federal Reserve Bank of Kansas City, 1988), 79-119.

Grossman, S. "Program Trading and Market Volatility: A Report on Intraday Relationship," *Financial Analyst Journal* (July/August 1988), 18-28.

Group of Thirty, "Clearance and Settlement Systems in World's Securities Markets," A Report by the Working Committee (1989).

Hamao, Y., R. W. Masulis, and V. Ng, "Correlations in Price Changes and Volatility Across International Stock Markets," *Review of Financial Studies* 3 (1990), 281-307.

Hamao, Y., R. W. Masulis, and V. Ng, "The Effects of the 1987 Stock Crash on International Financial Integration," forthcoming in *Japanese Financial Market Research* (Edited by W. Ziemba, W. Bailey, and Y. Hamao)(Amsterdam: North-Holland, 1991).

Hardouvelis, G., "Margin Requirements, Volatility, and the Transitory Components of Stock Prices," *American Economic Review* (September 1990), 736-62.

Hardouvelis, G., "Margin Requirements and Stock Market Volatility," *FRBNY Quarterly Review* (Summer 1988), 80-89.

Hardouvelis, G. and S. Peristiani, 1990, "Do Margin Requirements Matter? Evidence from US and Japanese Stock Markets," *FRBNY Quarterly Review* (Winter 1989-90), 16-35.

HKFE Clearing Corporation Limited, "Memorandum and Articles of Association of the HKFE Clearing Corporation Limited," (1989).

HKFE Clearing Corporation Limited, "Rules of the HKFE Clearing Corporation Limited," (March 1989).

HKFE Clearing Corporation Limited, "HKFE Clearing Corporation Limited Procedural Manual," (March 1989).

Hong Kong Securities Clearing Company Limited, "Consultative Paper on the Share Registration System under the Central Clearing and Settlement System (CCASS)" (1989).

Hong Kong Securities Clearing Company Limited, "Overview of the Central Clearing and Settlement System," (1989).

Hong Kong Securities Clearing Company Limited, "Preliminary System Design of the Central Clearing and Settlement System," (1989).

Hong Kong Securities Clearing Company Limited, "Consultative Paper on Business Operations and System Design of the Central Clearing and Settlement System (CCASS)" (March 1991).

Hong Kong Securities & Futures Commission, *Annual Report*, 1989.

Hopewell, M. H. and A. L. Schwartz, Jr., "Stock Price Movement Associated with Temporary Trading Suspensions: Bear Market versus Bull Market," *Journal of Financial and Quantitative Analysis* (November 1976), 577-90.

Howe, J. S. and G. G. Schlarbaum, "SEC Trading Suspensions: Empirical Evidence," *Journal of Financial and Quantitative Analysis* (September 1986), 323-33.

Hsieh, D. A. and M. H. Miller, "Margin Regulation and Stock Market Volatility," *Journal of Finance* (March 1990), 3-29.

Hsu, S. T., "Taiwan Stock Exchange in 1990." Paper delivered at the Fourth Annual Asia Capital Market Conference held in Bangkok, Thailand, on 17th June 1991.

International Organisation of Securities Commissions, *Capital Adequacy Standards for Securities Firms*, A Report of the Technical Committee of the International Organisation of Securities Commissions (1989).

International Society of Securities Administrators, "Symposium Report of Fourth International Symposium of Securities Administrators" (May 1988).

International Stock Exchange, *Quality of Markets Quarterly* (Winter 1987/1988).

Kabir, R., "Trading Suspensions on Stock Exchange: An Empirical Examination," Tilburg University Working Paper (1991) to be presented at the Third Annual Pacific-Basin Finance Conference in Seoul, Korea, in June 1991.

Kane, E. J., "Incentive Conflict in the International Regulatory Agreement on Risk-Based Capital," in *Pacific-Basin Capital Markets Research* Volume II (edited by S. G. Rhee and R. P. Chang) (Amsterdam, Netherlands: North-Holland, 1991), 3-21.

Kelleher, J. "The International Transmission of Stock Price Disruption in October 1987," *FRBNY Quarterly Review* (Summer 1988), 17-33.

Kessler, J. R., "Risks in the Clearing and Settlement Systems of Markets for Financial Futures and Options," *Risk Management in the Financial Services Industry*, OECD Publications (1992).

Kessler, J. R., "Study on Improvements in the Settlement of Cross-Border Securities Transactions in the European Economic Community," A Study for the Commission of the European Economic Community, Directorate-General XV, Financial Institutions and Company Law (1988).

King, M. A. and S. Wadhwani, "Transmission of Volatility Between Stock Markets," *Review of Financial Studies* 3 (1990), 5-33.

Korea Stock Exchange, *Korea Stock Exchange* (1990).

Korea Stock Exchange, *Fact Books*, 1987-1990.

Kuala Lumpur Stock Exchange, *Annual Reports*, 1987-1989.

Kuala Lumpur Stock Exchange, *Fact Books*, 1987-1989.

Kuala Lumpur Stock Exchange, "Information Paper on Proposed Central Depository System (CDS)" (1990).

Kuala Lumpur Stock Exchange, "Central Depository System (CDS): An Introduction for the Market Professional" (1990).

Kuala Lumpur Stock Exchange, *Memorandum and Articles of Association and Related Rules* (1991).

Kupiec, P., "Futures Margins and Stock Price Volatility: Is There Any Link?" Federal Reserve Board Working Paper No. 104 (January 1990).

Largay, J., "100% Margins: Combating Speculation in Individual Security Issues," *Journal of Finance* (September 1973), 973-86.

Leung, Iris C. W., "Clearing & Settlement Systems in Asia-Pacific Markets and Their Future Development," A Report of the Stock Exchange of Hong Kong (January 1991).

Luckett, D. G., "On the Effectiveness of the Federal Reserve's Margin Requirements," *Journal of Finance* (June 1982), 783-95.

Ma, C., R. P. Rao, and R. S. Sears, "Volatility, Price Resolution, and the Effectiveness of Price Limits," in *Regulatory Reform of Stock and Futures Markets* (Edited by F. R. Edwards)(Norwell, Mass: Kluwer Academic Publishers Group, 1989), A Special Issue of *Journal of Financial Services Research* (1989), 165-99.

McMillan, H. and J. Overdahl, "NYSE Rule 80A: An Evaluation of Its Effect on Trading Costs and Intermarket Linkage," US S.E.C. Working Paper (March 1991).

Mann, R. P. and G. Sofianos, "'Circuit Breakers' for Equity Markets," in *Market Volatility and Investor Confidence* (New York Stock Exchange, 1990), E1-E34.

Melamed, L., "Additional View of Panel Members," in *Market Volatility and Investor Confidence* (New York: New York Stock Exchange, 1990), H1 1-2.

Miller, M. H., "Volatility, Episodic Volatility and Coordinated Circuit-Breakers," in *Pacific-Basin Capital Markets Research* Volume II (Edited by S. G. Rhee and R. P. Chang) (Amsterdam: North-Holland, 1991), 23-47.

Miller, M. H., "Additional View of Panel Members," in *Market Volatility and Investor Confidence* (New York: New York Stock Exchange, 1990), H2 1-2.

Monetary Authority of Singapore, *Annual Reports*, 1987-1990.

Morris, C. S., "Coordinating Circuit Breakers in Stock and Futures Markets," *Federal Reserve Bank of Kansas City Economic Review* (March/April 1990), 35-48.

New York Stock Exchange, *Annual Reports*, 1987-1989.

New York Stock Exchange, *Fact Books*, 1988-1990.

New York Stock Exchange, "The Rule 80A Index Arbitrage Tick Test: Interim Report to the US Securities & Exchange Commission" (January 1991).

Ng, V. K., R. P. Chang, and R. Y. Chou, "An Examination of the Behavior of Pacific-Basin Market Volatility," in *Pacific-Basin Capital Markets Research* Volume II (edited by S. G. Rhee and R. P. Chang) (Amsterdam, Netherlands: North-Holland, 1991), 245-60.

O'Connor, S., "Systemic Risk in Securities Markets: A Concept in Search of a Definition," A Report to the Ad Hoc Group of Experts on Securities Markets of the Organisation for Economic Co-operation and Development (1989).

Organisation for Economic Co-operation and Development, *Systemic Risks in Securities Markets*, A Report by OECD Ad Hoc Group of Experts on Securities Markets (1991).

Park, J. and A. M. Fatemi, "The Linkages Between the Equity Markets of Pacific-Basin Countries and Those of the US, U.K., and Japan: A Vector Autoregression (VAR) Analysis," to be presented at the Third Annual Pacific-Basin Finance Conference to be held in Seoul, Korea on 3rd-5th June 1991.

Phadoongsidhi, M., "Settlement Procedure of the Stock Exchange of Thailand," (February 1991).

Presidential Task Force on Market Mechanisms, "Report of the Presidential Task Force on Market Mechanisms," A Report submitted to the President of the United States, the Secretary of the Treasury, and the Chairman of the Federal Reserve Board (1988).

Roll, R. W., "The International Crash of October 1987," in *Black Monday and the Future of Financial Markets* (Edited by R. W. Kamphuis, Jr., R . C. Kormendi, and J. W. Henry Watson) (Homewood, Illinois: Irwin, 1989), 35-70.

Salinger, M. A., "Stock Market Margin Requirements and Volatility: Implications for regulation of Stock Index Futures," in *Regulatory Reform of Stock and Futures Markets* (Edited by F. R. Edwards)(Norwell, Mass: Kluwer Academic Publishers Group, 1989), A Special Issue of *Journal of Financial Services Research* (1989), 121-38.

Sato, M., "Impact of the Futures Market on the Stock Market," in *Pacific-Basin Capital Markets Research* Volume II (Edited by S. G. Rhee and R. P. Chang) (Amsterdam: North-Holland, 1991), 85-95.

Schwert, G. W., "Margin Requirements and Stock Volatility," in *Regulatory Reform of Stock and Futures Markets* (Edited by F. R. Edwards)(Norwell, Mass: Kluwer Academic Publishers Group, 1989), A Special Issue of *Journal of Financial Services Research* (1989), 153-64.

Schwert, G. W., "Stock Market Volatility," *Financial Analysts Journal* (May/June 1990), 23-34.

Securities & Futures Commission, *Annual Report*, 1990.

Securities Review Committee, "The Operation and Regulation of the Hong Kong Securities Industry" (May 1988).

Singapore International Monetary Exchange Limited, *Annual Reports*, 1987-1989.

Singapore International Monetary Exchange Limited, *New Rules*, April 1990.

Sofianos, G., "Margin Requirements on Equity Instruments," *FRBNY Quarterly Review* (Summer 1988), 47-60.

Stock Exchange of Hong Kong Limited, *Annual Reports*, 1987-1990.

Stock Exchange of Hong Kong Limited, *Fact Books*, 1988-1989.

Stock Exchange of Singapore Limited, *Fact Books*, 1987-1989.

Stock Exchange of Singapore Limited, *Annual Reports*, 1987-1989.

Stock Exchange of Singapore Limited, *Memorandum & Articles of Association and Rules* (1991).

Stock Exchange of Singapore Limited, *By-Laws* (1991).

Stock Exchange of Thailand, *Fact Books*, 1987-1989.

Stock Exchange of Thailand, *SET Automated Project Functional Specification* Volume I (February 1991).

Stoll, H. R. and R. E. Whaley, "Stock Market Structure and Volatility," *Review of Financial Studies* 3 (1990), 37-71.

Taiwan Securities and Exchange Commission, *Annual Reports*, 1988-1990.

Taiwan Securities Central Depository, "Introductions on TSCD" (Undated).

Taiwan Securities Central Depository Co., Ltd., "Regulations Governing Securities Centralised Depository Enterprises" (1990).

Taiwan Securities Central Depository Co., Ltd., "Rule Governing the Book-Entry Operation of Securities in Centralised Custody" (1990).

Taiwan Securities Central Depository Co., Ltd., "Rule of Business Operation of Taiwan Securities Centralised Depository Company" (1990).

Taiwan Stock Exchange Corporation, *Taiwan Stock Exchange* (1990).

Taiwan Stock Exchange Corporation, *Fact Books*, 1987-1989.

Taiwan Stock Exchange Corporation, *Annual Reports*, 1987-1989.

Taiwan Stock Exchange Corporation, "Overview of Computer-Assisted Trading System at Taiwan Stock Exchange" (1990).

Telser, L. G., "October 1987 and the Structure of Financial Markets: An Exorcism of Demons," in *Black Monday and the Future of Financial Markets* (Edited by R. W. Kamphuis, Jr., R. C. Kormendi, and J. W. Henry Watson)(Homewood, Illinois: Irwin, 1989), 101-11.

Tokyo Stock Exchange, *Fact Book* 1990.

US Commodity Futures Trading Commission, Report on Stock Index Futures and Cash Market Activity During October 1989 to the US Commodity Futures Trading Commission," Division of Economic Analysis (May 1990).

US Commodity Futures Trading Commission, "Final Report on Stock Index Futures and Cash Market Activity During October 1987," Report by Division of Economic Analysis and Division of Trading and Markets (1988).

US Securities and Exchange Commission, "Trading Analysis of October 13 and 16, 1989," Report by Division of Market Regulation (1990).

Organisations Visited by the Author

Hong Kong

Securities & Futures Commission (SFC);
Monetary Affairs Branch;
Stock Exchange of Hong Kong Limited (SEHK);
Hong Kong Securities Clearing Co., Ltd. (HKSCC); and
Hong Kong Futures Exchange Ltd. (HKFE).

Korea

Ministry of Finance (MOF);
Securities & Exchange Commission (SEC); and
Korea Stock Exchange (KSE).

Malaysia

Bank Negara Malaysia;
Cagamas Berhad;
Capital Issues Committee (CIC);
Kuala Lumpur Stock Exchange (KLSE); and
Securities Clearing Automated Network Services Sdn. Berhad (SCANS).

Singapore

Monetary Authority of Singapore (MAS);
Stock Exchange of Singapore (SES); and
Singapore International Monetary Exchange Limited (SIMEX).

Thailand

      Ministry of Finance (MOF);
      Bank of Thailand (BOT); and
      Stock Exchange of Thailand (SET).

      Additionally, the author received generous co-operation from the following organisations in Taiwan which provided access to up-to-date information regarding the Taiwan securities market.

Taiwan

      Securities Exchange Commission (SEC); and
      Taiwan Stock Exchange Corporation (TSEC).

Appendix

The Microstructure of Asian Equity Markets

by

S. Ghon Rhee, Rosita P. Chang, and Roy Ageloff

1. Introduction

The countries in the Asian-Pacific region, as a group, have been enjoying the highest economic growth rate in the world. The combined market value of the region's common equities accounts for approximately one-third of the world's total capital market volume. The strategic importance of capital markets in this region for international investment decisions is well demonstrated by the increasing number of mutual funds specialising in Asian equities. It is also demonstrated by the phenomenal success of many closed-end investment companies including the Asia Pacific Fund [1], the Korea Fund [25], the Korea-Europe Fund [26], the Malaysia Fund [31], the Taiwan Fund [40], and the Thai Fund [41] in the US and London capital markets.

One of the most significant international financial developments of the 1980s has been the gradual opening of the capital markets of Asian-Pacific countries to the outside world. In September 1987, the Securities Exchange of Thailand set up an Alien Board to facilitate trading of Thai securities among foreign investors as part of its effort to open the Thai market. Starting in August 1989, foreign investors have been allowed to exchange their Korean convertible bonds into stocks, which has opened the door for direct foreign ownership of Korean blue-chip firms such as Samsung Electronics Co., Daewoo Heavy Industries Co., Yukong Ltd., and Gold Star Co. [27]. In 1991, foreign brokerage houses were allowed to join the Korea Stock Exchange as members through establishing joint ventures with Korean firms. Currently, 25 foreign securities firms are active members of the Tokyo Stock Exchange while trading by foreign investors of Japanese shares amounted to 17 per cent of total trading value in 1989. Beginning in 1991, foreign institutional investors are allowed to invest directly in Taiwan Stock Exchange listed securities within the preliminary maximum limit of US $2.5 billion.

Table 1 **Market size** (As of December 1989)

Country	Number of firms listed	Domestic firms	Foreign firms	Total market capitalisation (US$ billion)	
Hong Kong	298	284	14	$77.6	(1.61%)
Indonesia	56	56	0	$2.5	(0.04%)
Japan	1 716	1 597	119	$4 260.4	(88.21%)
Korea	626	626	0	$140.5	(2.91%)
Malaysia	307	251	56	$39.6	(0.82%)
Philippines	144	144	0	$11.6	(0.24%)
Singapore	333	136	197	$35.9	(0.74%)
Taiwan	181	181	0	$235.9	(4.88%)
Thailand	175	175	0	$25.7	(0.53%)
Total	3 836	3 450	386	$4 829.7	(100.00%)
NYSE	1 720	1 633	87	$3 029.7	

Table 2 **Trading volume** (As of December 1989)

Country	Trading volume (US$ billion)		Turnover ratio*
Hong Kong	$34.6	(0.96%)	44.59%
Indonesia	$0.5	(0.01%)	20.00%
Japan	$2 431.2	(67.20%)	57.07%
Korea	$120.9	(3.34%)	86.05%
Malaysia	$18.5	(0.51%)	46.72%
Philippines	$1.3	(0.04%)	11.21%
Singapore	$20.6	(0.56%)	57.38%
Taiwan	$976.2	(26.98%)	413.82%
Thailand	$14.7	(0.41%)	57.20%
Total	$3 618.0	(100.00%)	74.92%
NYSE	$1 542.8		52.00%

* the turnover ratio is defined as the ratio of trading volume to market capitalisation.

In spite of their economic growth and important role in the world trade, it has only been in recent years that the Asian capital markets have received any attention from academic researchers. Most of these, however, have concentrated on Japan. The topics studied include the small firm effect, the price/earnings ratio effect, the January effect, and the day-of-the-week pattern of daily stock returns. (See [4], [20], [21], [23], [29], and [32], among others.) More recent papers move beyond addressing stock market anomalies to examine fundamental issues such as the normality of return distribution [2], the return and volume variance effect [3], rights offering [22], IPOs [24,45], and cross market volatility [34]. This new set of studies broadens the range of research topics, and is an encouraging development in the research on Asian markets. These studies stimulate further research in not only Japan, but also in other countries in the region.

This study examines the microstructure of the Asian equity markets. It is intended to enhance an understanding of each of the major stock exchanges in Asia by presenting their profiles and current status. This paper is divided under several headings including:

(1) Market size;
(2) Trading value and turnover ratio;
(3) Stock market indices;
(4) Market performance;
(5) P/E ratios and dividend yields;
(6) Brokerage fees and other transaction costs;
(7) Trading hours and trading days;
(8) Foreign exchange control and foreign ownership; and
(9) Withholding tax rates for foreign investors.

2. Market size

At the end of 1989, a total of 3 836 firms was listed on the major stock exchanges of nine Asian-Pacific countries including Hong Kong, Indonesia, Japan, Korea, Malaysia, the Philippines, Singapore, the Taiwan and Thailand. Total market capitalisation amounted to $4 829.7 billion. This amount is 2.58 times as large as the New York Stock Exchange's market capitalisation. As shown in Table 1, the market capitalisation of the Tokyo Stock Exchange was $4,260.4 billion, accounting for 88.21 per cent of the entire Asian equity markets. Next in order are Taiwan with 4.88 per cent, Korea with 2.91 per cent, and Hong Kong with 1.61 per cent (See [7], [8], [9], [10], [11], [12], [13], [14], [15], [32], [33], [38], [41], and [42].)

Table 3 **Asian stock market indices** (As of December 1989)

Country	Index name	Base date	Base index	Composition	Supplementary indices
Hong Kong	Hong Kong Index (HKI)	04/02/1986	1 000	49	6 Industry indices
Indonesia	Composite Share Price Index	08/10/1982	100	All listed firms	None
Japan	Tokyo Stock Price Index (TOPIX)	01/04/1968	100	First section stocks	A. Section indices B. Indices by firm size C. 28 Industry indices
Korea	Korea Composite Stock Price Index (KCSPI)	01/04/1980	100	All listed firms	A. Section indices B. Indices by firm size C. 34 Industry indices
Malaysia	KLSE Composite	1977	100	83	6 Industry indices
Philippines	MSE Composite Price Index	01/02/1985	100	25	3 Industry indices
Singapore	S.E.S. All-Share Index	1975	100	All listed firms	6 Industry indices
Taiwan	Weighted Stock Price Index	01/01/1966	100	All listed firms	A. 2 Section indices B. 8 Industry indices
Thailand	SET Index	04/30/1975	100	All listed firms	5 Industry indices

Of the 3 836 firms listed on the Asian exchanges, 3 450 firms were domestic and the remaining 386 firms were foreign firms. The number of firms reported for Japan includes the Tokyo Stock Exchange-listed firms only. There are seven other independent exchanges in Japan located in Osaka, Nagoya, Kyoto, Hiroshima, Fukuoka, Niigata, and Sapporo. Tokyo Stock Exchange, the largest among the seven, has 79 per cent of all listed companies in Japan and has 97 per cent of the market value. Of the 1 597 firms, 945 domestic firms were cross-listed between the Tokyo Stock Exchange and the remaining seven exchanges, while 652 firms were listed only on the Tokyo Stock Exchange. However, 422 firms were listed not on the Tokyo Stock Exchange but on the remaining seven exchanges. Indonesia and the Philippines are the other two countries in the region which have multiple exchanges. There are two stock exchanges in Indonesia, the Jakarta Stock Exchange and Surabaya Stock Exchange. In the Philippines, there are the Manila Stock Exchange and the Makati Stock Exchange. In both countries, the securities are required to be cross-listed. The reported market capitalisation for Indonesia and the Philippines represent those of the Jakarta Stock Exchange and the Manila Stock Exchange, respectively.

3. Trading value and turnover ratio

In 1989, the total annual trading value of the nine Asian-Pacific countries was US$3 618.5 billion, which is 2.36 times that of New York Stock Exchange. Tokyo Stock Exchange accounted for 67.19 per cent of the total trading value, followed by Taiwan with 26.98 per cent and Korea with 3.34 per cent.[1] In terms of turnover ratio, Taiwan has the highest turnover ratio of 413.82 per cent, followed by Korea with 86.05 per cent, and Singapore with 57.38 per cent. It is amazing that, even though Taiwan Stock Exchange accounted for only 4.88 per cent of the combined market capitalisation in the region, it had 27 per cent of the combined trading value, making the Taiwan Stock Exchange one of the busiest stock exchanges in the world.

4. Stock market indices

Table 3 summarises background information concerning stock market indices computed by the stock exchanges of nine countries. All the indices are calculated using the market-value-weighted formula as defined by:

Current index = (current AMV/base AMV) x base index,

where AMV stands for the aggregate market value. The base index and base date vary from one exchange to another. Comparable indices in the United States are the Standard & Poor's Composite Indices and New York Stock Exchange Common Stock Indices. For the purpose of maintaining the continuity of the reported index numbers, the base AMV must be adjusted for: (a) new listings; (b) delistings; (c) rights offerings; (d) public offerings; (e) private placements; (f) mergers; (g) exercises of warrants; and (h) conversions of convertible securities into common stock.

Table 4 Summary statistics of Asian market portfolio returns (per cent)
(January 1980 - December 1989)

Country	In local currency	In US dollars	
	mean	mean	exchange gain
Hong Kong	0.98	0.59	-0.40
Japan	1.53	1.97	0.37
Korea	1.84	1.56	-0.30
Malaysia	0.46	0.11	-0.15
Philippines	0.78	-0.12	-1.00
Singapore	0.50	0.57	0.09
Taiwan	2.39	2.66	0.25
Thailand	1.48	1.29	-0.21
Mean* 1.55	1.93	0.32	
NYSE	-	0.99	-

Note: * The market-capitalisation-weighted average

Table 5 Summary statistics of Asian market portfolio risk
(January 1980 - December 1989)

Country	In local currency returns			In US dollars returns		
	Total risk	β		Total risk	β	Exchange risk
Hong Kong	0.1032	0.86	(4.71)*	0.1100	0.87	(4.48)*	0.0170
Japan	0.0413	0.37	(5.09)*	0.0585	0.32	(2.99)*	0.0357
Korea	0.0607	0.20	(1.73)	0.0645	0.17	(1.39)	0.0201
Malaysia	0.0915	0.93	(5.97)*	0.0968	0.97	(5.80)*	0.0142
Philippines	0.0957	0.25	(1.35)	0.1040	0.26	(1.32)	0.0460
Singapore	0.0672	0.72	(6.48)*	0.0710	0.75	(6.28)*	0.0161
Taiwan	0.1120	0.61	(2.92)*	0.1168	0.61	(2.82)*	0.0193
Thailand	0.0623	0.49	(4.38)*	0.0637	0.48	(4.26)*	0.0194
NYSE	-	-		0.0480	1.00		-

Notes: 1.   Figures in ( ) are t-values.
            2.   * indicates statistical significance at $\alpha = 1$ per cent.

Table 3 shows the major composite index, base date, base index value, and its composition. The major composite index is supplemented by sub-indices as well as other composite indices.[2] For example, in addition to the Tokyo Stock Price Index (TOPIX), which covers 1,136 stocks listed in the First Section, the Tokyo Stock Exchange computes a composite index called the Second Section Stock Price Index covering 446 stocks listed on its Second Section.[3] The TSE's First Section comprises the larger listed shares which meet the listing criteria while the Second Section shares are relatively new on the exchange and those issued by smaller firms.[4] Additionally, the TOPIX sub-indices for 28 industry groups and three indices for large, medium, and small size firms are also computed and published [41].[5] Another popular index in Japan is the Nikkei-Dow Average Share Price Index, which is computed on a formula similar to the Dow-Jones Industrial Average [36]. The computation method of stock market indices of Korea, Taiwan, and Thailand is identical to that of the TOPIX indices. (See [10], [11], and [13].)

The Stock Exchange of Hong Kong Ltd. adopted a new composite index called the Hong Kong Index (HKI) on 2nd April 1986 after consolidating the Far East Stock Exchange Limited, the Hong Kong Stock Exchange, the Kam Ngan Stock Exchange Ltd., and the Kowloon Stock Exchange. The HKI is computed using 49 constituent blue-chip stocks selected from six representative industries in Hong Kong. Another popular index, the Hang Seng Index, is computed by the Hang Seng Bank Ltd. It is composed of 33 constituent stocks which include four finance stocks, six utilities, nine properties, and 14 commerce & industrials. Of the 33 stocks in the Hang Seng Index, 31 of them are included in the HKI.[6] (See [7] and [18].)

5. Market performance

Table 4 presents summary statistics on monthly returns of market portfolios of nine Asian-Pacific countries. It covers the ten-year period from January 1980 to December 1989. All major stock market indices introduced in the previous section were used for computation except Hong Kong. The Hang Seng Index was used for Hong Kong because the new Hong Kong Index was established in 1986.

The performance of Asian equity markets has far exceeded that of the US market as measured by the Standard & Poor's 500 Composite Index.[7] For example, the US stock market registered an average monthly return of 0.99 per cent during the ten-year study period. Over the same period, the nine Asian equity markets yielded a market-capitalisation-weighted average local currency return of 1.55 per cent per month.

Table 6 Correlation matrix: local currency return
(January 1980 - December 1989)

	Japan	Korea	Malaysia	Philippines	Singapore	Taiwan	Thailand	USA.
Hong Kong	0.28*	0.10	0.45*	0.19†	0.46*	0.25*	0.34*	0.40*
Japan		0.27*	0.28*	0.02	0.28*	0.32*	0.19†	0.42*
Korea			0.10	0.19†	0.12	-0.04	-0.11	0.16
Malaysia				0.08	0.97*	0.37*	0.38*	0.51*
Philippines					0.10	-0.19†	0.02	0.12
Singapore						0.37*	0.40*	0.53*
Taiwan							0.52*	0.26*
Thailand								0.37*

Note: * indicates statistical significant at α = 1 per cent
† indicates statistical significant at α = 5 per cent

Table 7 Correlation matrix: US dollar return
(January 1980 - December 1989)

	Japan	Korea	Malaysia	Philippines	Singapore	Taiwan	Thailand	USA.
Hong Kong	0.23†	0.09	0.44*	0.19†	0.46*	0.23†	0.29*	0.38*
Japan		0.27*	0.19	0.09	0.22†	0.12	0.02	0.27*
Korea			0.04	0.20†	0.07	- 0.01	- 0.03	0.13
Malaysia				0.15	0.97*	0.41*	0.39*	0.51*
Philippines					0.15	-0.16	0.06	0.12
Singapore						0.33*	0.40*	0.51*
Taiwan							0.49*	0.25*
Thailand								0.36*

Note: * indicates statistical significant at α = 1 per cent
† indicates statistical significant at α = 5 per cent

The average return in US dollars of the Asian markets amounted to 1.93 per cent. Of this amount, monthly foreign exchange gain was 0.32 per cent. In terms of local currency return, the performance of the Taiwan market portfolio is the best with an average return of 2.39 per cent, followed by Korea with 1.84 per cent, Japan with 1.53 per cent, and Thailand with 1.48 per cent. When measured in returns of US dollars, Taiwan, Japan, and Korea are the top three performers, with respective monthly returns of 2.66 per cent, 1.97 per cent, and 1.56 per cent. The returns on Taiwan and Japanese market portfolios were augmented by the respective foreign exchange gain of 0.25 per cent and 0.37 per cent per month. In contrast, the Korean won depreciated against US dollars by 0.30 per cent per month, and the Thai baht depreciated by 0.21 per cent per month.

These phenomenally high returns have not been achieved without risk. The total risk of investments in Asian equity markets, as measured by the standard deviation of local currency returns, is on average, 1.5 times greater than that of the US market. As indicated in Table 5, the market portfolios of Hong Kong, Malaysia, the Philippines, and Taiwan, have standard deviations at least twice as large as the US market portfolio. During the study period, Japan was the only country with a smaller standard deviation than the US, 0.0413 vs. 0.0480. Total risk of Asian market portfolio returns in US dollars is larger than the total risk measured using the local currency returns. For example, total risk rises from 0.0413 to 0.0585 as the yen-denominated returns are converted into US dollar-denominated returns. The difference between the two, 0.0172, is the contribution of currency risk. However, note from the last column that the exchange risk as measured by standard deviation of the rate of change in spot rates is greater than this difference. The exchange risk of Japanese yen is 0.0357. This indicates that more than half of the exchange risk is eliminated by the diversification effect. This would be true when portfolio returns in local currency have low correlations with the rates of change in spot exchange rates. Usually, the observed correlations between the two are very low, and sometimes even negative. For example, the estimated correlation between returns on the market portfolio in Japanese yen and the rates of change in the yen value is only 0.18.

Also reported in Table 5 are β estimates of each country's market portfolio. They are estimated using a market model in which monthly local currency returns, as well as US dollar returns, on each country's market portfolio are regressed on the US market portfolio's returns. The estimated β's when local currency returns are used, ranging from Korea's 0.20 to Malaysia's 0.93. All the β estimates except for Korea and the Philippines are significant at $\alpha = 1$ per cent level. The estimated β's increase slightly when the US dollar returns are used for the regressions. The results strongly indicate that the correlation between each of Asian markets and the US market is fairly low.

Table 8 P/E ratios and dividend yields
(As of December 1989)

Country	P/E ratio (times)	Dividend Yield (per cent)
Hong Kong	10.76	6.05%
Indonesia	63.80	5.30%
Japan	70.60	0.45%
Korea	14.30	2.00%
Malaysia	36.22	2.02%
Philippines	12.50	4.78%
Singapore	15.80	n.a.
Taiwan	55.91	1.58%
Thailand	26.39	2.07%
NYSE	15.00	3.20%

Table 9 Brokerage fees and other costs
(As of December 1989)

Country	For investment of US$10 000	For investment of US$100 000
Hong Kong	$61.40$136.60 (a)	$605.91 $1 355.91 (a)
Indonesia	$100.30	$1 003.00
Japan	$115.78	$816.96
Korea	$66.30	$663.00
Malaysia	$140.00 (b)	$1 400.00 (b)
Philippines	$175.00	$1 750.00
Singapore	$115.00	$1 200.00
Taiwan	$14.25	$142.50
Thailand	$50.00	$500.00

Notes: (a)   Stockbrokers in Hong Kong may charge a fee of not less than 0.25 per cent, but not more than 1 per cent of the value of the transaction.

(b)   The brokerage fee varies depending upon the price per share in Kuala Lumpur. For the convenience of illustration, it is assumed that the share is priced at M$1.00 or above.

Tables 6 and 7 report the correlation between the Asian markets and the US market. Table 6 shows the correlation matrix when local currency returns on each of the Asian market portfolios are used. Indonesia is excluded due to an incomplete set of observations. The last column indicates the correlations between the Asian markets and the US market. The lowest correlation of 0.12 is obtained for the Philippines, while the highest correlation of 0.53 is observed for Singapore. The correlations among Asian markets are also relatively low. This implies a good potential for risk diversification. The only exception is the correlation of 0.97 observed between Singapore and Malaysia, which is not surprising in light of the large number of cross-listed firms. The correlations between Japan and the remaining Asian countries are surprisingly low. Thus, the percentage of common variance among the Asian markets is extremely small despite their geographical proximity.

Table 7 reports the correlation matrix when monthly returns in US dollars are used. In most cases, the estimated correlation coefficients are smaller than those reported in Table 6. Nevertheless, the relative independence of the Asian and US markets is clearly suggested by both tables. Without the market crash in October 1987 which triggered world stock markets to move together for a while, the correlations could have been much smaller than reported.[8]

6. P/E Ratios and dividend yields

Table 8 presents price earnings (P/E) ratios and dividend yields of each country. In 1989, the Tokyo Stock Exchange reported the highest P/E ratio of 70.60, followed by Indonesia with 63.80, Taiwan with 55.91, and Malaysia with 36.22. The P/E ratio of the NYSE-listed shares was 15.00. The lowest P/E ratio of 10.76 was reported from Hong Kong. P/E ratios of Korea and the Philippines were also relatively low.

In terms of dividend yields, Hong Kong and Thailand reported high dividend yields of 6.05 per cent and 5.30 per cent, respectively. The average dividend yield of the NYSE stocks was 3.20 per cent. In contrast, low dividend yields were observed for Japan with 0.45 per cent and Taiwan with 1.58 per cent. Two reasons may be cited for this trend: (a) many Asian firms maintain a dividend policy under which a fixed percentage of the par value is paid as dividend; and (b) stock prices had been steadily going up in the past few years.

7. Brokerage fees and other transaction costs

Table 9 summarises brokerage fees applicable to each of the nine Asian-Pacific countries. For ease of comparison, the brokerage fees in US dollars are estimated assuming total investments of US$10 000 and US$100 000, respectively. Whenever relevant information is available, other transaction costs including stamp taxes, exchange taxes, registration fees, etc., are included. For an investment of $10 000, transaction costs range from $14.25 in Taiwan to $175 in the Philippines. For a larger investment of $100 000, Malaysia is the most costly, while Taiwan is the least costly. Low transaction costs in Taiwan explain why the Taiwan Stock Exchange is one of the busiest in the world. Investors in Thailand and Korea also enjoy relatively low transaction costs.

Table 10 **Trading hours and trading days**
(As of December 1989)

Country	Trading hours		Weekly trading hours	Trading Days
Hong Kong	M-F:	10:00 am - 12:30 pm 2:30 pm - 3:30 pm	17-1/2 hours	246 days
Indonesia	M-F:	10:00 am - 12:00 noon	10 hours	247 days
Japan	M-F:	9:00 am - 11:00 am 1:00 pm - 3:00 pm	22 hours	249 days
Korea	M-F: Sat:	9:40 am - 11:40 am 1:20 pm - 3:20 pm 9:40 am - 11:40 am	22 hours	289 days
Malaysia	M-F:	10:00 am - 11:00 am, 11:15 am - 12:30 pm 2:30 pm - 4:00 pm	18-3/4 hours	244 days
Philippines	M-F:	9:30 am - 12:00 noon	12-1/2 hours	244 days
Singapore	M-F:	10:00 am - 12:30 pm, 2:30 pm - 4:00 pm	20 hours	250 days
Taiwan	M-F: Sat:	9:00 am - 12:00 noon 9:00 am - 11:00 am	17 hours	287 days
Thailand	M-F:	9:30 am - 11:30 am	10 hours	247 days
NYSE	M-F:	9:30 am - 4:00 pm	32-1/2 hours	252 days

8. Trading hours and trading days

Based upon trading hours summarised in Table 10, the following scenario can be drawn. At 7 p.m., eastern standard time (EST), in the United States, the Tokyo Stock Exchange begins trading, followed by the Korea Stock Exchange at 7:40 p.m., the Taiwan Stock Exchange at 8 p.m., and the Manila Stock Exchange at 8:30 p.m., respectively. At 9 p.m., stock exchanges in Hong Kong, Kuala Lumpur, and Singapore will be open. The Stock Exchange of Thailand and the Jakarta Stock Exchange will be the last to open at 9:30 p.m. and 10 p.m., respectively. The first ones to close are stock exchanges in Kuala Lumpur and Singapore at 3 a.m., EST. All exchanges in Asia have short trading hours, ranging from 2 hours to 4 hours, in contrast to 6-1/2 hours of trading at the New York Stock Exchange. As of December 1989, the Korea Stock Exchange and Taiwan Stock Exchange are the only two exchanges in Asia conduct business on Saturdays. The trading days for each Asian exchanges range from 289 days for Korea to 244 days in Malaysia, the Philippines and Singapore.

9. Foreign exchange control and foreign ownership

The accessibility of US investors to the Asian equity markets is determined by two major factors: (a) foreign exchange control and (b) limitation on foreign ownership. The nine Asian countries may be classified into four categories depending upon the degree of government control over foreign exchange and foreign ownership, as is summarised in Table 11 [17].

Korea and Taiwan are expected to allow foreigners to invest in domestic securities in 1991. Currently, foreign investors can have indirect access to local markets only through purchase of shares issued by authorised mutual funds or closed-end investment companies. Since October 1981, the Korean government allowed five mutual funds and two closed-end investment companies to be launched for portfolio investment in Korean securities by non-residents. Under similar arrangements, four investment companies had been introduced for foreign investors who wanted to have access to the Taiwan market. Although foreign investors have direct access to the Thai capital market, there are eight investment companies participating in the Thai market and a few more waiting for approval from government authorities.

Table 11 Control of foreign exchange and foreign ownership
(As of December 1989)

Country	Foreign exchange control	Restriction on foreign ownership	Category
Hong Kong	None	None	1
Indonesia	None for normal investment portfolio activities	None for 49 per cent ownership or less	3
Japan	None	None except industries in "national interest"	2
Korea	Yes but being liberalised	Severely restricted	4
Malaysia	None for normal investment portfolio activities	None for 15 per cent ownership or less	3
Philippines	Yes but fairly liberal for normal Investment portfolio activities	None for 40 per cent ownership or less via "B" class shares	3
Singapore	None	None except limits on selected domestic firms	2
Taiwan	Yes on in-bound foreign capital	Severely restricted	4
Thailand	Yes but fairly liberal	a. None for 25 per cent ownership or less in commercial banks b. None for 50 per cent ownership or less in others c. Foreigners trade on Alien Board only	3

Category 1:   The laissez-faire economy, where neither exchange control nor any limitations regarding ownership of domestic firms by foreign investors exists. Hong Kong is the only market in this category.

Category 2:   The capital markets are fully liberalised except for restrictions on selective industries and/or firms in "national interest." Japan and Singapore may be classified in this category. Both countries do not have foreign exchange control and, in general, there is no limitation on the acquisition of domestic firms by foreigners except those firms/industries so designated by the government.

Category 3:   The capital markets are substantially open but not completely liberalised. Indonesia, Malaysia, the Philippines, and Thailand belong to this category. Usually, foreign exchange controls do not exist or they are minimal for normal investment portfolio activities. However, foreign ownership of domestic firms is limited to a fixed percentage of the shares outstanding or of voting right.[9]

Category 4:   The capital markets are in the process of being opened. Foreign exchange controls exist and foreign investors do not have direct access to local equity markets. Korea and Taiwan are in this category. Some foreigners do have stakes in domestic firms through joint venture or direct foreign investment approved by the government.

10. Withholding tax rates for foreign investors

Table 12 summarises withholding tax rates on dividends, interest, and capital gains in the nine Asian countries. Three countries have bilateral tax treaties with the US [16]. As a result, low withholding tax rates are applicable for US investors in Japan, Korea, and the Philippines. Hong Kong, Malaysia, and Singapore do not impose dividend income taxes although no bilateral tax treaties exist. Most of Asian nations do not penalise investors, foreign as well as domestic, on capital gains from normal portfolio investment operations, exception for Thailand. Among the non-tax treaty countries, withholding tax rate on interest is highest in Singapore at 33 per cent. Thailand comes next with a 25 per cent tax rate on interest. Indonesia and Malaysia impose a 20 per cent withholding tax rate.

11. Conclusion

The capital markets studied in this paper offer solid long-term investment opportunities as each country in the region is in the process of introducing a series of changes in economic policies which favor the private sector and deregulate its market. Each country has been making good progress in privatising government-owned corporations and in gradual deregulation of financial sector of its economy. As a result, personal and institutional of investors will have greater interests in the Asian capital markets as an alternative to mature markets in the United States and European countries. A systematic research effort is warranted for a better and comprehensive understanding of the region's capital markets.

Table 12 **Withholding tax rates or foreign investors**
(As of December 1989)

Country	Dividend		Interest		Capital Gain
Hong Kong	0%		a. 0% if paid by financial institutions b. 16.5% if paid by others		0%
Indonesia	20%		20%		Lack of information
Japan	Foreign investors:	20%	Foreign investors:	20%	Not taxable except gains derived from frequent and large transactions
	US investors:	15%	US investors:	15%	
Korea	Foreign investors:		Foreign investors:		Taxable unless exempted under tax treaty.
	a. Public corp b. Others	10% 25%	a. Bank interest b. Others	10% 25%	
	US investors:	15%	US investors:	12%	0%
Malaysia	0%		20%		0%
Philippines	Foreign investors: US investors:	35% 35%	Foreign investors: US investors:	20% 15%	0.25% based upon the gross selling price
Singapore	0%		33%		0%
Taiwan	a. 35% b. 20% for foreign investment approved banks by the government		a. 20% b. 0% on interest paid by		0%
Thailand	20%		25%		25%

Notes

1. The Tokyo Stock Exchange handled 86.1 per cent of the total trading value in Japan, followed by Osaka with 10.8 per cent and Nagoya with 2.7 per cent

2. The formula for Indonesia's Composite Share Price Index is not available to us.

3. At the Tokyo Stock Exchange, foreign stocks are assigned to the foreign section while domestic stocks are assigned to either the first or second section. As of December 1989, 1 136 firms are listed on the First Section, 446 firms on the Second Section, 119 firms on the Foreign Section.

4. Assignment of listed firms to the First or Second Section depends upon multiple criteria for (a) the scale of business, (b) the liquidity of the securities, (c) trading volume, (d) business results, etc.

5. It is interesting to note that the size of firms is determined by the number of shares listed:

   a. Large firms have 200 million or more shares listed.

   b. Medium firms have 60 million or more shares but under 200 million shares listed.

   c. Small firms have less than 60 million shares listed.

6. Unfortunately, no sufficient information is available about the composite share price index of Indonesia.

7. The use of the S&P 500 Composite Index is justified because (a) all foreign market indices are value-weighted, and (b) no dividend reinvestments are taken into account.

8. Bailey, Stulz, and Yen [2] suggest that significant departure from the random walk hypothesis may produce downward bias in the estimated correlations between daily returns on Asian market portfolios and those on US market portfolios.

9. The Securities Exchange of Thailand set up the Alien Board in September 1987 to facilitate trading securities by foreigners for the issues which had reached the maximum statutory or voluntary limit of foreign ownership. The Manila Stock Exchange, on the

91

other hand, introduced two classes of shares--Class A and Class B. Foreign investors are allowed to buy and sell Class B shares but not Class A shares. Interestingly, a price differential is observed for the same firm's issue between the Regular Board and Alien Board in Bangkok. This differential also exists in Manila between Class A shares and Class B shares issued by the same firm.

References

[1] The Asia Pacific Fund, Inc.: *Preliminary Prospectus*, September 1986.

[2] Bailey, W., Stulz, R. M., and Yen, S., 1990, Properties of Daily Stock Returns from the Pacific Basin Stock Markets: Evidence and Implications, *Pacific-Basin Capital Markets Research*, Volume I, (edited by S. G. Rhee and R. P. Chang), (Amsterdam: Elsevier Science Publishers B. V.), 155-171.

[3] Barclay, M. J., Litzenberger, R. H. and Warner, J. B., 1988, Private Information, Trading Volume, and Stock Return Variance, University of Rochester Working Paper presented at the First Annual Pacific-Basin Finance Conference.

[4] Brown, P. Keim, D. B., Kleidon, A. W., and Marsh, T. A., 1983, Stock Return Seasonalities and the Tax-Loss-Selling Hypothesis, *Journal of Financial Economics* 12, 105-127.

[5] *Capital Market Development in the Asia-Pacific Region*: Summary of the Proceedings and Papers Presented at a Symposium Held on 14-16 January 1986 in Manila, Philippines (Manila: Asian Development Bank, 1986).

[6] *Capital Market Development in Selected Developing Member Countries of the Asian Development Bank* (Manila: Asian Development Bank, 1985).

[7] *Fact Book 1989* (Hong Kong: The Stock Exchange of Hong Kong Ltd., 1989).

[8] *Fact Book* (Jakarta: The Indonesian Capital Market, Capital Market Executive Agency, Ministry of Finance, Republic of Indonesia, 1988).

[9] *Fact Book 1990* (New York: The New York Stock Exchange, 1990).

[10] *Fact Book* (Seoul: The Korea Stock Exchange, May 1990).

[11] *Fact Book '90* (Bangkok: The Securities Exchange of Thailand, 1990).

[12] *Fact Book 1990* (Singapore: The Stock Exchange of Singapore, 1990).

[13] *Fact Book 1989* (Taipei: The Taiwan Stock Exchange, 1990).

[14] *Fact Book 1990* (Tokyo: The Tokyo Stock Exchange, 1990).

[15] *Fact Book 1989* (Tokyo: The Tokyo Stock Exchange, 1989).

[16] *Foreign and U.S. Corporate Income and Withholding Tax Rates* (New York: Ernst & Whinney, 1988).

[17] *Foreign Exchange Rates and Restrictions* (New York: Ernst & Whinney, 1988).

[18] *Hang Seng Index Fact Sheet*, Economic Research Department, Hang Seng Bank Ltd., July 1984.

[19] *Investors' Information Guide*, Manila Stock Exchange, 1988.

[20] Jaffe, J. and Westerfield, R., 1985, Patterns in Japanese Common Stock Returns: Day of the Week and Turn of the Year Effects, *Journal of Financial and Quantitative Analysis* 20, 261-272.

[21] Chou, S. and Johnson, K. H., 1990, An Empirical Analysis of Stock Market Anomalies: Evidence from the Republic of China in Taiwan, *Pacific-Basin Capital Markets Research*, Volume I, (edited by S. G. Rhee and R. P. Chang), (Amsterdam: Elsevier Science Publishers B. V.), 283-312.

[22] Kang, H., 1990, Effects of Seasoned Equity Offerings in Korea on Shareholder's Wealth, *Pacific-Basin Capital Markets Research*, Volume I, (edited by S. G. Rhee and R. P. Chang), (Amsterdam: Elsevier Science Publishers B. V.), 265-282.

[23] Kato, K. and Schalheim, J. S., 1985, Seasonal and Size Anomalies in the Japanese Stock Market, *Journal of Financial and Quantitative Analysis* 20, 243-259.

[24] Kim, E. H. and Lee, Y. K., 1990, Issuing Stocks in Korea, *Pacific-Basin Capital Markets Research*, Volume I, (edited by S. G. Rhee and R. P. Chang), (Amsterdam: Elsevier Science Publishers B. V.), 243-253.

[25] The Korea Fund, Inc.: *Prospectus*, April 1986.

[26] The Korea-Europe Fund Limited: *Prospectus*, March 1987.

[27] *Korea Stock Exchange* (Seoul: The Korea Stock Exchange, October 1988).

[28] *The Kuala Lumpur Stock Exchange Annual Reports*, 1990.

[29] Lee, I., Pettit, R. R., and Swankoski, M. V., 1989, Daily Return Relationship among Asian Stock Markets, University of Houston Working Paper presented at the First Annual Pacific-Basin Finance Conference.

[30] Ma, T. and Shaw, T. Y., 1989, The Relationship between Market Value, P/E Ratio, Trading Volume and the Stock Return of Taiwan Stock Exchange, *Pacific-Basin Capital Markets Research*, Volume I, (edited by S. G. Rhee and R. P. Chang), (Amsterdam: Elsevier Science Publishers B. V.), 313-335.

[31] The Malaysia Fund, Inc.: *Prospectus*, May 1987.

[32] *Manila Stock Exchange Annual Report*, 1990.

[33] *Manila Stock Exchange Annual Report*, 1989.

[34] Ng, V. K., Chang, R. P., and Chou, R. Y., 1991, An Examination of the Behavior of Pacific-Basin Stock Market Volatility, forthcoming in *Pacific-Basin Capital Markets Research*, Volume II, (edited by S. Rhee and R. Chang), (Amsterdam: Elsevier Science Publishers B.V.).

[35] Rhee, S. G., Chang, R. P., and Ageloff, R., 1990, An Overview of Equity Markets in Pacific-Basin Countries, *Pacific-Basin Capital Markets Research*, Volume I, (edited by S. G. Rhee and R. P. Chang), (Amsterdam: Elsevier Science Publishers B. V.), 81 100.

[36] *Securities Markets in Asia and Oceania* (Tokyo: The Asian Securities' Analysts Council, May 1982).

[37] *The SES All-Share Price Indices*, 1975-August 1988, The Stock Exchange of Singapore Ltd.

[38] Statistical Supplement: *Supplement to the Fact Book of the Indonesian Capital Market*, Capital Market Executive Agency, Ministry of Finance, Republic of Indonesia, 1988.

[39] The Taiwan Fund: Placing Memorandum, December 1984.

[40] The Thai Fund, Inc.: *Prospectus*, December 1986.

[41] Tokyo Stock Exchange, Comparative Statistical Table of East Asia Stock Exchanges, presented at IXth EASEC Meeting, Manila, December 1990.

[42] Tokyo Stock Exchange, Commissions and Other Costs of East Asian Stock Exchanges, presented at IXth EASEC Meeting, Manila, December 1990.

[43] *TOPIX: Tokyo Stock Price Index* (Tokyo: The Tokyo Stock Exchange, June 1988).

[44] *What Do You Know About The Hong Kong Index?* (Hong Kong: The Hong Kong Stock Exchange, May 1988).

[45] Wethyavivorn, K. and Koo-smith, Y., 1991, Initial Public Offers in Thailand, 1988-1989: Price and Return Patterns, forthcoming in *Pacific-Basin Capital Markets Research*, Volume II, (edited by S. Rhee and R. Chang), (Amsterdam: Elsevier Science Publishers B.V.).

MAIN SALES OUTLETS OF OECD PUBLICATIONS – PRINCIPAUX POINTS DE VENTE DES PUBLICATIONS DE L'OCDE

Argentina – Argentine
Carlos Hirsch S.R.L.
Galería Güemes, Florida 165, 4° Piso
1333 Buenos Aires   Tel. (1) 331.1787 y 331.2391
                           Telefax: (1) 331.1787

Australia – Australie
D.A. Book (Aust.) Pty. Ltd.
648 Whitehorse Road, P.O.B 163
Mitcham, Victoria 3132   Tel. (03) 873.4411
                               Telefax: (03) 873.5679

Austria – Autriche
OECD Publications and Information Centre
Schedestrasse 7
D-W 5300 Bonn 1 (Germany)   Tel. (49.228) 21.60.45
                                Telefax: (49.228) 26.11.04

Gerold & Co.
Graben 31
Wien I   Tel. (0222) 533.50.14

Belgium – Belgique
Jean De Lannoy
Avenue du Roi 202
B-1060 Bruxelles   Tel. (02) 538.51.69/538.08.41
                          Telefax: (02) 538.08.41

Canada
Renouf Publishing Company Ltd.
1294 Algoma Road
Ottawa, ON K1B 3W8   Tel. (613) 741.4333
                                Telefax: (613) 741.5439
Stores:
61 Sparks Street
Ottawa, ON K1P 5R1   Tel. (613) 238.8985
211 Yonge Street
Toronto, ON M5B 1M4   Tel. (416) 363.3171
Federal Publications
165 University Avenue
Toronto, ON M5H 3B8   Tel. (416) 581.1552
                                Telefax: (416)581.1743
Les Éditions La Liberté Inc.
3020 Chemin Sainte-Foy
Sainte-Foy, PQ G1X 3V6   Tel. (418) 658.3763
                                Telefax: (418) 658.3763

China – Chine
China National Publications Import
Export Corporation (CNPIEC)
P.O. Box 88
Beijing   Tel. 44.0731
                                Telefax: 401.5661

Denmark – Danemark
Munksgaard Export and Subscription Service
35, Nørre Søgade, P.O. Box 2148
DK-1016 København K   Tel. (33) 12.85.70
                                Telefax: (33) 12.93.87

Finland – Finlande
Akateeminen Kirjakauppa
Keskuskatu 1, P.O. Box 128
00100 Helsinki   Tel. (358 0) 12141
                                Telefax: (358 0) 121.4441

France
OECD/OCDE
Mail Orders/Commandes par correspondance:
2, rue André-Pascal
75775 Paris Cédex 16   Tel. (33-1) 45.24.82.00
                                Telefax: (33-1) 45.24.85.00
                                or (33-1) 45.24.81.76
                                Telex: 620 160 OCDE
Bookshop/Librairie:
33, rue Octave-Feuillet
75016 Paris   Tel. (33-1) 45.24.81.67
                                (33-1) 45.24.81.81
Librairie de l'Université
12a, rue Nazareth
13100 Aix-en-Provence   Tel. 42.26.18.08
                                Telefax: 42.26.63.26

Germany – Allemagne
OECD Publications and Information Centre
Schedestrasse 7
D-W 5300 Bonn 1   Tel. (0228) 21.60.45
                                Telefax: (0228) 26.11.04

Greece – Grèce
Librairie Kauffmann
Mavrokordatou 9
106 78 Athens   Tel. 322.21.60
                                Telefax: 363.39.67

Hong Kong
Swindon Book Co. Ltd.
13 - 15 Lock Road
Kowloon, Hong Kong   Tel. 366.80.31
                                Telefax: 739.49.75

Iceland – Islande
Mál Mog Menning
Laugavegi 18, Pósthólf 392
121 Reykjavik   Tel. 162.35.23

India – Inde
Oxford Book and Stationery Co.
Scindia House
New Delhi 110001   Tel.(11) 331.5896/5308
                                Telefax: (11) 332.5993
17 Park Street
Calcutta 700016   Tel. 240832

Indonesia – Indonésie
Pdii-Lipi
P.O. Box 269/JKSMG/88
Jakarta 12790   Tel. 583467
                                Telex: 62 875

Ireland – Irlande
TDC Publishers – Library Suppliers
12 North Frederick Street
Dublin 1   Tel. 74.48.35/74.96.77
                                Telefax: 74.84.16

Israel
Electronic Publications only
Publications électroniques seulement
Sophist Systems Ltd.
71 Allenby Street
Tel-Aviv 65134   Tel. 3-29.00.21
                                Telefax: 3-29.92.39

Italy – Italie
Libreria Commissionaria Sansoni
Via Duca di Calabria 1/1
50125 Firenze   Tel. (055) 64.54.15
                                Telefax: (055) 64.12.57
Via Bartolini 29
20155 Milano   Tel. (02) 36.50.83
Editrice e Libreria Herder
Piazza Montecitorio 120
00186 Roma   Tel. 679.46.28
                                Telex: NATEL I 621427
Libreria Hoepli
Via Hoepli 5
20121 Milano   Tel. (02) 86.54.46
                                Telefax: (02) 805.28.86
Libreria Scientifica
Dott. Lucio de Biasio 'Aeiou'
Via Meravigli 16
20123 Milano   Tel. (02) 805.68.98
                                Telefax: (02) 80.01.75

Japan – Japon
OECD Publications and Information Centre
Landic Akasaka Building
2-3-4 Akasaka, Minato-ku
Tokyo 107   Tel. (81.3) 3586.2016
                                Telefax: (81.3) 3584.7929

Korea – Corée
Kyobo Book Centre Co. Ltd.
P.O. Box 1658, Kwang Hwa Moon
Seoul   Tel. 730.78.91
                                Telefax: 735.00.30

Malaysia – Malaisie
Co-operative Bookshop Ltd.
University of Malaya
P.O. Box 1127, Jalan Pantai Baru
59700 Kuala Lumpur
Malaysia   Tel. 756.5000/756.5425
                                Telefax: 757.3661

Netherlands – Pays-Bas
SDU Uitgeverij
Christoffel Plantijnstraat 2
Postbus 20014
2500 EA 's-Gravenhage   Tel. (070 3) 78.99.11
Voor bestellingen: Tel. (070 3) 78.98.80
                                Telefax: (070 3) 47.63.51

New Zealand – Nouvelle-Zélande
GP Publications Ltd.
Customer Services
33 The Esplanade - P.O. Box 38-900
Petone, Wellington   Tel. (04) 5685.555
                                Telefax: (04) 5685.333

Norway – Norvège
Narvesen Info Center - NIC
Bertrand Narvesens vei 2
P.O. Box 6125 Etterstad
0602 Oslo 6   Tel. (02) 57.33.00
                                Telefax: (02) 68.19.01

Pakistan
Mirza Book Agency
65 Shahrah Quaid-E-Azam
Lahore 3   Tel. 66.839
                                Telex: 44886 UBL PK. Attn: MIRZA BK

Portugal
Livraria Portugal
Rua do Carmo 70-74
Apart. 2681
1117 Lisboa Codex   Tel.: (01) 347.49.82/3/4/5
                           Telefax: (01) 347.02.64

Singapore – Singapour
Information Publications Pte. Ltd.
Pei-Fu Industrial Building
24 New Industrial Road No. 02-06
Singapore 1953   Tel. 283.1786/283.1798
                                Telefax: 284.8875

Spain – Espagne
Mundi-Prensa Libros S.A.
Castelló 37, Apartado 1223
Madrid 28001   Tel. (91) 431.33.99
                                Telefax: (91) 575.39.98
Libreria Internacional AEDOS
Consejo de Ciento 391
08009 - Barcelona   Tel. (93) 488.34.92
                                Telefax: (93) 487.76.59
Llibreria de la Generalitat
Palau Moja
Rambla dels Estudis, 118
08002 - Barcelona   Tel. (93) 318.80.12 (Subscripcions)
                      (93) 302.67.23 (Publicacions)
                      Telefax: (93) 412.18.54

Sri Lanka
Centre for Policy Research
c/o Colombo Agencies Ltd.
No. 300-304, Galle Road
Colombo 3   Tel. (1) 574240, 573551-2
                                Telefax: (1) 575394, 510711

Sweden – Suède
Fritzes Fackboksföretaget
Box 16356
Regeringsgatan 12
103 27 Stockholm   Tel. (08) 23.89.00
                                Telefax: (08) 20.50.21
Subscription Agency/Abonnements:
Wennergren-Williams AB
Nordenflychtsvägen 74
Box 30004
104 25 Stockholm   Tel. (08) 13.67.00
                                Telefax: (08) 618.62.32

Switzerland – Suisse
OECD Publications and Information Centre
Schedestrasse 7
D-W 5300 Bonn 1 (Germany)   Tel. (49.228) 21.60.45
                                Telefax: (49.228) 26.11.04
Suisse romande
Maditec S.A.
Chemin des Palettes 4
1020 Renens/Lausanne   Tel. (021) 635.08.65
                                Telefax: (021) 635.07.80
Librairie Payot
6 rue Grenus
1211 Genève 11   Tel. (022) 731.89.50
                                Telex: 28356
Subscription Agency – Service des Abonnements
Naville S.A.
7, rue Lévrier
1201 Genève   Tél.: (022) 732.24.00
                                Telefax: (022) 738.87.13

Taiwan – Formose
Good Faith Worldwide Int'l. Co. Ltd.
9th Floor, No. 118, Sec. 2
Chung Hsiao E. Road
Taipei   Tel. (02) 391.7396/391.7397
                                Telefax: (02) 394.9176

Thailand – Thaïlande
Suksit Siam Co. Ltd.
113, 115 Fuang Nakhon Rd.
Opp. Wat Rajbopith
Bangkok 10200   Tel. (662) 251.1630
                                Telefax: (662) 236.7783

Turkey – Turquie
Kültur Yayinlari Is-Türk Ltd. Sti.
Atatürk Bulvari No. 191/Kat. 21
Kavaklidere/Ankara   Tel. 25.07.60
Dolmabahce Cad. No. 29
Besiktas/Istanbul   Tel. 160.71.88
                                Telex: 43482B

United Kingdom – Royaume-Uni
HMSO
Gen. enquiries   Tel. (071) 873 0011
Postal orders only:
P.O. Box 276, London SW8 5DT
Personal Callers HMSO Bookshop
49 High Holborn, London WC1V 6HB
                                Telefax: 071 873 2000
Branches at: Belfast, Birmingham, Bristol, Edinburgh,
                                         Manchester

United States – États-Unis
OECD Publications and Information Centre
2001 L Street N.W., Suite 700
Washington, D.C. 20036-4910   Tel. (202) 785.6323
                                Telefax: (202) 785.0350

Venezuela
Libreria del Este
Avda F. Miranda 52, Aptdo. 60337
Edificio Galipán
Caracas 106   Tel. 951.1705/951.2307/951.1297
                     Telegram: Libreste Caracas

Yugoslavia – Yougoslavie
Jugoslovenska Knjiga
Knez Mihajlova 2, P.O. Box 36
Beograd   Tel. (011) 621.992
                                Telefax: (011) 625.970

Orders and inquiries from countries where Distributors have
not yet been appointed should be sent to: OECD Publications Service, 2 rue André-Pascal, 75775 Paris Cédex 16,
France.

Les commandes provenant de pays où l'OCDE n'a pas
encore désigné de distributeur devraient être adressées à :
OCDE, Service des Publications, 2, rue André-Pascal, 75775
Paris Cédex 16, France.

OECD PUBLICATIONS, 2 rue André-Pascal, 75775 PARIS CEDEX 16
PRINTED IN FRANCE
(21 92 01 1) ISBN 92-64-13638-X - No. 45913 1992